MW01078799

Tom Loeser Photography
310-351-3024

Jack!
Enjoy the ride

Tom Loeser

THE ART OF MOPAR

CHRYSLER, DODGE, AND PLYMOUTH MUSCLE CARS

Brimming with creative inspiration, how-to projects, and useful information to enrich your everyday life, Quarto Knows is a favorite destination for those pursuing their interests and passions. Visit our site and dig deeper with our books into your area of interest: Quarto Creates, Quarto Cooks, Quarto Homes, Quarto Lives, Quarto Drives, Quarto Explores, Quarto Gifts, or Quarto Kids.

© 2017 Quarto Publishing Group USA Inc.
Text © 2017 Tom Glatch
Photography © 2017 Tom Loeser

First published in 2017 by Motorbooks, an imprint of The Quarto Group, 401 Second Avenue North, Suite 310, Minneapolis, MN 55401 USA.
T (612) 344-8100 F (612) 344-8692 www.QuartoKnows.com

All rights reserved. No part of this book may be reproduced in any form without written permission of the copyright owners. All images in this book have been reproduced with the knowledge and prior consent of the artists concerned, and no responsibility is accepted by producer, publisher, or printer for any infringement of copyright or otherwise, arising from the contents of this publication. Every effort has been made to ensure that credits accurately comply with information supplied. We apologize for any inaccuracies that may have occurred and will resolve inaccurate or missing information in a subsequent reprinting of the book.

Motorbooks titles are also available at discount for retail, wholesale, promotional, and bulk purchase. For details, contact the Special Sales Manager by email at specialsales@quarto.com or by mail at The Quarto Group, Attn: Special Sales Manager, 401 Second Avenue North, Suite 310, Minneapolis, MN 55401 USA.

10 9 8 7 6 5 4 3 2

ISBN: 978-0-7603-5249-6

Library of Congress Cataloging-in-Publication Data

Names: Glatch, Tom, 1956- author.
Title: Art of Mopar : Chrysler, Dodge, and Plymouth muscle cars / Tom Glatch.
Description: Minneapolis, MN : Quarto Publishing Group USA, Inc., [2017]
Identifiers: LCCN 2016045006 | ISBN 9780760352496 (hc w/jacket)
Subjects: LCSH: Chrysler automobile. | Muscle cars--United States.
Classification: LCC TL215.C55 G54 2017 | DDC 629.2220973--dc23
LC record available at https://lccn.loc.gov/2016045006

Acquiring Editor: Darwin Holmstrom
Project Manager: Jordan Wiklund
Art Director: James Kegley
Layout: Kim Winscher

On the endpapers: 1963 Plymouth Sport Fury Super Stock 426 (front); 2016 Dodge Challenger SRT Hellcat (back).
On the front cover: 1970 Dodge Charger R/T Hemi.
On the back cover: 1970 Dodge Challenger T/A.
On the frontis: 1972 Plymouth Road Runner GTX 440+6 engine detail.
On the title page: 1966 Dodge Coronet 426 Hemi.

Printed in China

MIX
Paper from responsible sources
FSC® C104723

THE ART OF **MOPAR**

CHRYSLER, DODGE, AND PLYMOUTH MUSCLE CARS

TOM GLATCH /// PHOTOGRAPHY BY TOM LOESER

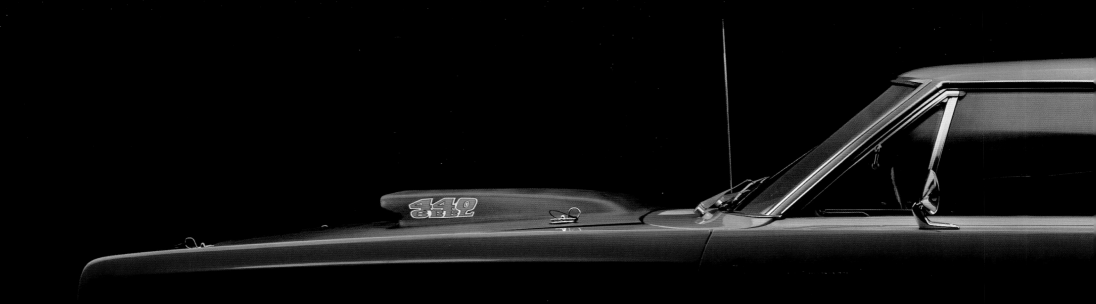

CONTENTS

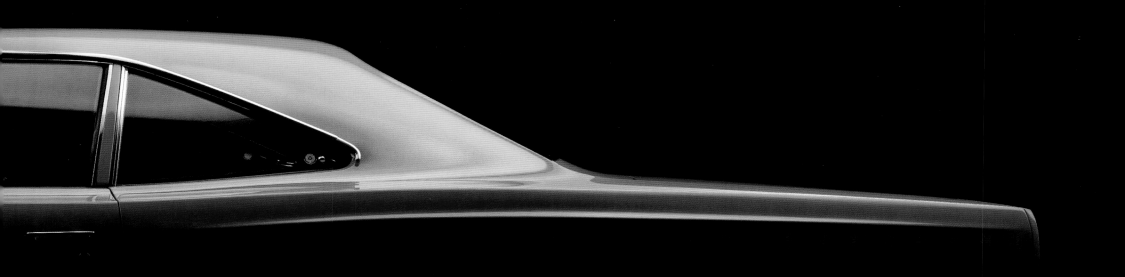

AUTHOR'S ACKNOWLEDGMENTS

Beginning in the earliest days of the internet, Dr. John Zatz had the presence of mind to capture interviews, articles, and talks by former Chrysler employees on his allpar.com site. Frank Peiler and the staff at *Collectible Automobile* magazine also began interviewing prominent designers, engineers, and other contributors to American automobile development many years ago. With so many of the people who were involved in the famous Chrysler cars of the 1960s and 1970s no longer with us, that makes the contributions of allpar.com and *Collectible Automobile* truly invaluable.

Many thanks to the great Chrysler designer Milt Antonick, who was able to clarify some small but important details. Also, the websites hamtramck-historical.com, aerowarriors.com, wwnboa.org, and maxwedge.com provide a service to the Mopar community that is immeasurable.

Most of all thanks to my wife, Kelly, who kept the home fires burning while I concentrated single-mindedly on this book; our son, Sean, who with his expertise in English assisted with the nuances of the language; and our daughter, Keara, and her husband, Brandan, (both gearheads) for their encouragement and enthusiasm.

Tom Glatch

PHOTOGRAPHER'S ACKNOWLEDGMENTS

Great thanks go first and foremost to The Brothers for once again opening the doors of their amazing automobile collection to me to study, select, and photograph. The collection they have built is without equal, as is their generosity.

Doug Dwyer and Marty Marr put in hundreds of hours cleaning and prepping the cars for my shoot. Their energy and enthusiasm are endless. I really appreciate their hard work and their friendship. For this book, Doug took on the role of assistant photographer, as well.

Early in the process of this book, Randy Leffingwell collaborated with me in the planning and vehicle selection. I'm grateful for his help.

A special *thank you* to Trisha Maas and Cineo Lighting for providing the specialized lighting equipment that I used to light-paint these beautiful cars. Thanks also to Silvio, owner of Silvio's Camera, for the generous equipment contributions to this project.

Last but far from least, I owe deep thanks to my wife, Susan, for her love, support, and patience during the long weeks I was away from home shooting these cars and the longer hours on the computer processing these images once I got home. I like cars but Susan is the love of my life.

Tom Loeser

INTRODUCTION

If cars could talk, my first car, a 1970 Plymouth Duster 340, could tell some tales. The parking lot of the Marc's Big Boy in West Allis, Wisconsin, in 1975 was more than impressive—it was downright intimidating. The front row of the lot, facing State Highway 100 (also known as Mayfair Road), was exclusively Mopars—two or three 1969 Road Runners, a '68 Charger, a 1969 'Cuda 440, a '70 GTX, and my Duster. Highway 100 was Milwaukee's equivalent of Detroit's Woodward Avenue, *the* place for a little street action, and my neighborhood friends and I ruled over that stretch of pavement with our Plymouths and Dodges. We didn't just park our rides there; we earned those honored parking places.

Though most of us grew up in GM or Ford families, we all were dedicated Chrysler fanatics. The reason was simple. Turn on the TV and there was Richard Petty's Plymouth or David Pearson's Dodge winning yet another NASCAR race on *Car and Track* or *Wide World of Sports*. Open up *Hot Rod* or *Motor Trend* and there was Ronnie Sox or The Ramchargers earning another Stock Eliminator crown. When we were old enough to start attending the USAC stock car races at the Milwaukee Mile, or go to Great Lakes Dragaway, we got to see, hear, and most definitely feel Hemi power up close. Henry Ford II may have spent millions winning the Indianapolis 500 or Le Mans, but for us that could have been on another planet. Yet over at Dodge City in Wauwatosa or HUB Chrysler Plymouth in West Allis, there were cars in the showroom not far removed from what our racing heroes were wheeling. No wonder when we could finally buy our first cars, it was Mopar or no car.

That's why this book is so special to me. Great automobiles have stories to tell, from a previous owner, or someone who made them famous, or the people who created them. This book tells the stories of twenty-five of the most incredible Dodge and Plymouth performance cars from The Brothers Collection. They have literally the best of the best, and photographer Tom Loeser used his light-painting technique to capture their striking beauty as only he can. It truly is an honor to tell these stories.

PART 1

RAPID

Good times, bad times, Chrysler had their share. In the course of just a few years, they went from being the most admired manufacturer in Detroit to the most ignored.

Chrysler hired Virgil Exner from General Motors to be their design chief, and the fruits of that acquisition hit the showrooms in 1955 as the first of the "Forward Look" Chryslers, Dodges, Plymouths, and DeSotos. Powered by the first-generation Hemi engines, the Chrysler 300 and Dodge D-500 were the fastest on the track and on the turnpike. By 1957 the lower, sleeker "Forward Look" Mopars stunned the competition, to the point that GM and Ford had to react quickly to update their offerings for '58 and '59.

But by 1960 the "Forward Look" looked anything but forward, and by the next year the DeSoto division was gone and the rest of the company was reeling. Exner's designs for 1961 were downright ugly, and the upcoming cars for '62 almost bizarre. The mood in Chrysler's Highland Park, Michigan, headquarters was somber. It was time to clean house.

Lynn Townsend was promoted from corporate controller to president of Chrysler Corporation in 1961. His background was accounting, but Townsend grew up in Michigan and understood the auto business. He also had teenage sons who would voice their opinions about Chrysler products.

Virgil Exner was fired in the fall of 1961, and Elwood Engle was hired away from Lincoln to direct the turnaround. Engel inherited a real mess, as the '62 cars were already in showrooms, and the '63s were already being tooled. To make matters worse, Chrysler's previous management decided that all of their full-sized Dodges and Plymouths would be downsized, thinking that was what America wanted. It wasn't, and potential buyers went elsewhere.

Change comes slowly in the automotive world. It can take months to design, engineer, tool, and produce even the smallest change to a vehicle; a fresh set of sheet metal or a new platform took huge investments of dollars and three years or more to accomplish. Yet Lynn Townsend was on the cover of *Time* magazine's December 26, 1962, issue: "The big increase in auto sales this fall contributed more than anything else to keeping the US prosperous; and one of the big contributors to the increase in auto sales was the long-ailing Chrysler Corp., which in the space of one year did a surprising turnaround. Thanks to the energetic leadership of its new president, Lynn Alfred Townsend, 43, Chrysler in 1962 was the comeback story of US business."

Still, the next few years would either save Chrysler, or seal its fate.

ACCELERATION

CHAPTER ONE

1963 PLYMOUTH SPORT FURY SUPER STOCK 426

PRODUCTION

86

OPTIONS

509 426 Max Wedge
($578.80)

3-Speed Manual
Transmission (N/C)

BB1 Ebony Paint

326 Red Vinyl Interior

HORSEPOWER

415 at 5,600 rpm

TORQUE

470 at 4,400 rpm

As a young engineer at Chrysler, Dick Maxwell could see the brand's problem first hand: "We were virtually invisible on the street." The exclusive and expensive Chrysler 300 "letter cars" still had some reputation for performance. Otherwise, the days of the Dodge D-500 and Plymouth Fury performance machines of the mid-fifties were long gone.

Other young Chrysler employees could see it too. Discussions began over lunch breaks, and in 1959 Dick Maxwell, Tom Hoover, Wayne Erickson, and other like-minded guys created the Ramchargers Racing Club. Completely independent of Chrysler Corporation, club members began working evenings and racing weekends. Some of their experiments in ram induction and exhaust design included

fabricating the first tunnel ram intake manifold. Their creations were truly cutting edge, and they took those innovations back to their day jobs at Chrysler. By late summer 1961 the Ramchargers Dodge was shocking the Super Duty Pontiacs, 409 Chevys, and 406 Fords.

In 1962 a group of like-minded Plymouth employees created the Golden Commandos. Like the Ramchargers, the Golden Commandos were volunteers independent of Chrysler, with backgrounds in all different aspects of Chrysler's business. By early 1963 one of their three Plymouths was runner-up at the 1963 Winternationals in Pomona, California. And like the Ramchargers, they took their findings back to their day jobs at Chrysler.

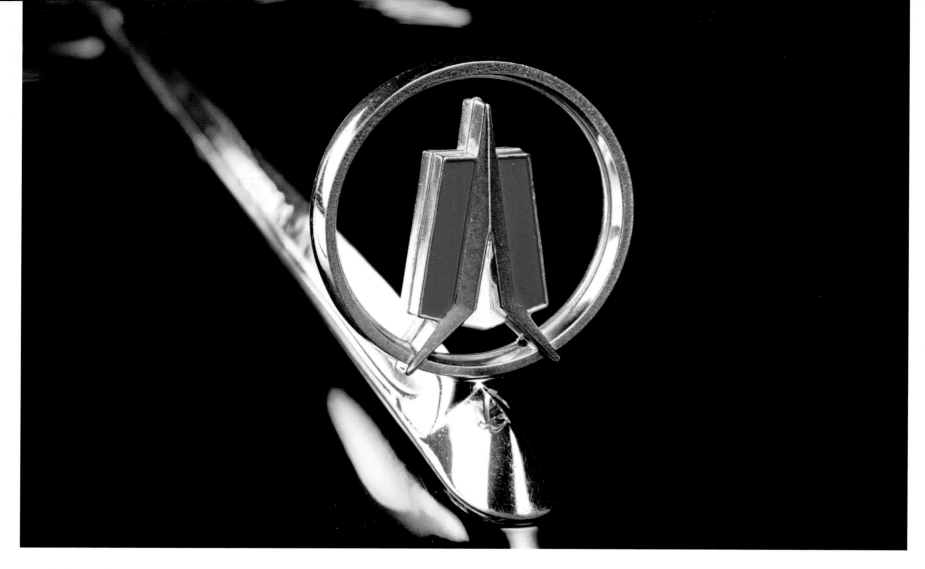

Whether Dodge or Plymouth, Chrysler products were highly visible on the drag strips in 1963. Back then the stars of drag racing were not the wild Top Fuel cars. Instead, the big events were the Top Stock Eliminator competitions, where seventy-five or more Super Stock racers would compete for the title, and Dodges and Plymouths often were leading the way. One key to their success was under the hood. Plymouth called it the Super Stock 426, Dodge the Ramcharger 426, but generically the engine was known as the Max Wedge. Available in two versions—one street/strip engine with 11.0:1 compression rated at 415 horsepower, the other a 13.5:1 compression race-only mill delivering 425 horsepower—the 426 Max Wedge was packed with nothing but premium racing components right from the factory. Twin Carter carburetors sat on a unique cross-ram manifold, and free-flowing cast-iron exhaust curved up over the heads and down to 3-inch pipes.

These powerful engines were stuffed into Dodges and Plymouths that maybe didn't look terribly stylish, but were smaller and, thanks to Chrysler's famed unit-body construction, lighter than the competition. As any engineer can tell you, the power-to-weight ratio is key to any racer's success, and these cars were superior. They also bucked the trend to racing with manual transmissions, preferring the tough A727 TorqueFlite automatic. "Racing these cars on seven-inch slicks was like driving on ice," said Tom Hoover, and the softer launch of an automatic helped the tires stay glued to the strip.

The best part of all this development was everything was available to the public. In 1963 Plymouth published their Super Stock brochure to show racers how to do it. "When the new Plymouth Super Stock 413 came out last May, I'll admit I was skeptical," wrote Tom Grove in the brochure. "I was a dyed-in-the-wool Chevy man, but in the speed business I had an open mind. . . . Our first 'Melrose Missile' was

down to 12.3 the first week we ran it in competition and we broke 13 records and won 11 trophies the first eight times we had it out." Tom Grove's *Melrose Missiles* became a mainstay of Plymouth drag racers for years to come.

Fenner-Tubbs Chrysler Plymouth, in Lubbock, Texas, wanted a racer to promote their dealership. They ordered this 1963 Sport Fury with the 415-horsepower Max Wedge 426 to do just that. Most racers bought the stripped-down Savoy model, which was the most basic of transportation geared toward government fleets and taxi services. Racers didn't need frills, and the Savoy was so Spartan a cigarette lighter was a $10.80 option. The fact that Fenner-Tubbs ordered a top-of-the-line Sport Fury indicates they probably displayed it in the showroom and used it on the street as well at the strip. The Sport Fury was ordered with the standard three-speed manual transmission, but sometime later a four-speed with Hurst shifter was added, which is exactly as it is now in The Brothers Collection. These cars were ridiculously fast, as *Hot Rod Magazine*, in the January 1963 issue, recorded a 12.69-second, 112-mile-per-hour quarter-mile. Today the Sport Fury shows only 38,870 miles on the odometer, many of those coming a quarter-mile at a time.

The 1963 Plymouths may have been a bit homely, but with Max Wedge power under the hood, they were no longer invisible.

"Climb into the driver's seat, settle back, punch the 'D' button and stab the

throttle. Presto, a 13-second standing ¼-mile with a trap speed of 110 mph!"

—*Car Life*

CHAPTER TWO

1965 PLYMOUTH CONVERTIBLE 426 WEDGE

PRODUCTION 21

OPTIONS

80 426 Wedge ($533.60)

365 TorqueFlite 3-Speed Automatic

331 Light Package ($11.65)

410 Power Steering ($84.35)

441 Power Brakes ($41.75)

443 AM/FM ($126.70)

512 Remote Controlled Mirror ($11.80)

TT1 Medium Red Metallic Paint

P4X Black Vinyl Interior

582 White Convertible Top

HORSEPOWER

365 at 4,800 rpm

TORQUE

470 at 3,200 rpm

Elwood Engle's designers were able to whip the '64 Plymouth Furys and Dodge Polaras into good sellers, and things were improving. Then Pontiac's "youth market" bombshell dropped in 1964, the performance GTO. True, the hot Max Wedge Mopars were the same size as the GTO, were on the market two years ahead of John DeLorean's creation, and were much faster, but they didn't have the attention-grabbing style and comfort of the GTO. Dodge and Plymouth were still playing catch-up.

The last year for the original B-body cars would be 1965. They were conceived to be a smaller full-sized sedan in 1962, but the market had evolved and they were squarely in the intermediate or midsized class, along with Ford's Fairlane and Mercury Comet, and GM's Olds Cutlass, Buick Special, Chevy Chevelle, and Pontiac Tempest, which included the car the magazines couldn't stop gushing over, the GTO. Where traditionally Dodges were considered more upscale than Plymouths, and rode on longer

wheelbases, for '65 the Dodge Coronet and Plymouth Belvedere were both 116 inches. That saved tooling and production costs. Both cars shared the same cowl, roof, and doors, but money was budgeted for each design studio to create front and rear sheet-metal and trim changes to differentiate the two brands. In a bit of automotive irony, designers were tasked in 1964 with making the midsized Fury look full-sized; now in 1965 they were supposed to take the exact same car and make it look midsized. "At the time we designed these, the guidance from sales was to make the cars look as wide as possible, front and rear," said designer John Samsen.

True full-sized cars, the new C-body Chryslers, Dodges, and Plymouths, hit the showrooms that year. Also new in 1965 was the Satellite, a Belvedere designed for the youth market. "A new way to swing without going out on a limb," said the Chrysler sales booklet. It looked the part, with minimal exterior chrome and spinner wheel covers. The interior was dressed up with bucket

Continued on page 25

We're big on volumetric efficiency.

That way, our engines stay out front. Along with our cars.

Take the Plymouth Belvedere Satellite above, with its high-performance Plymouth Commando 426 wedge-head V-8. That power plant is the street version of our competition-designed 426 Hemi engine, which holds more records than our competitors care to count.

The Plymouth Satellite's Commando 426 V-8 has high-performance valve springs, cam, pistons and plugs.

Hydraulic tappets, dual breaker distributor, nonsilenced air cleaner, dual exhausts, heavy-duty clutch. And 365 horsepower.

Choose: Satellite hardtop or Satellite convertible. Axles to your driving tastes. Standard engine: 273-cu.-in. V-8. Optional V-8's: The 318-, 361-, the 383-cubic-inchers. And, say we immodestly, the optional high-performance Plymouth Commando 426 V-8.

Standard on the Belvedere Satellite are front bucket seats, center console with glove box, Safety-Rim wheels, custom wheel covers with spinner hubs, torsion-bar suspension.

Volumetric efficiency. You can research that one further. Or you can just tool on down to where they're giving free Plymouth Satellite rides. That one's a little easier to find.

THE ROARING '65s
FURY
BELVEDERE
VALIANT
BARRACUDA

Plymouth

PLYMOUTH DIVISION ★ **CHRYSLER** MOTORS CORPORATION

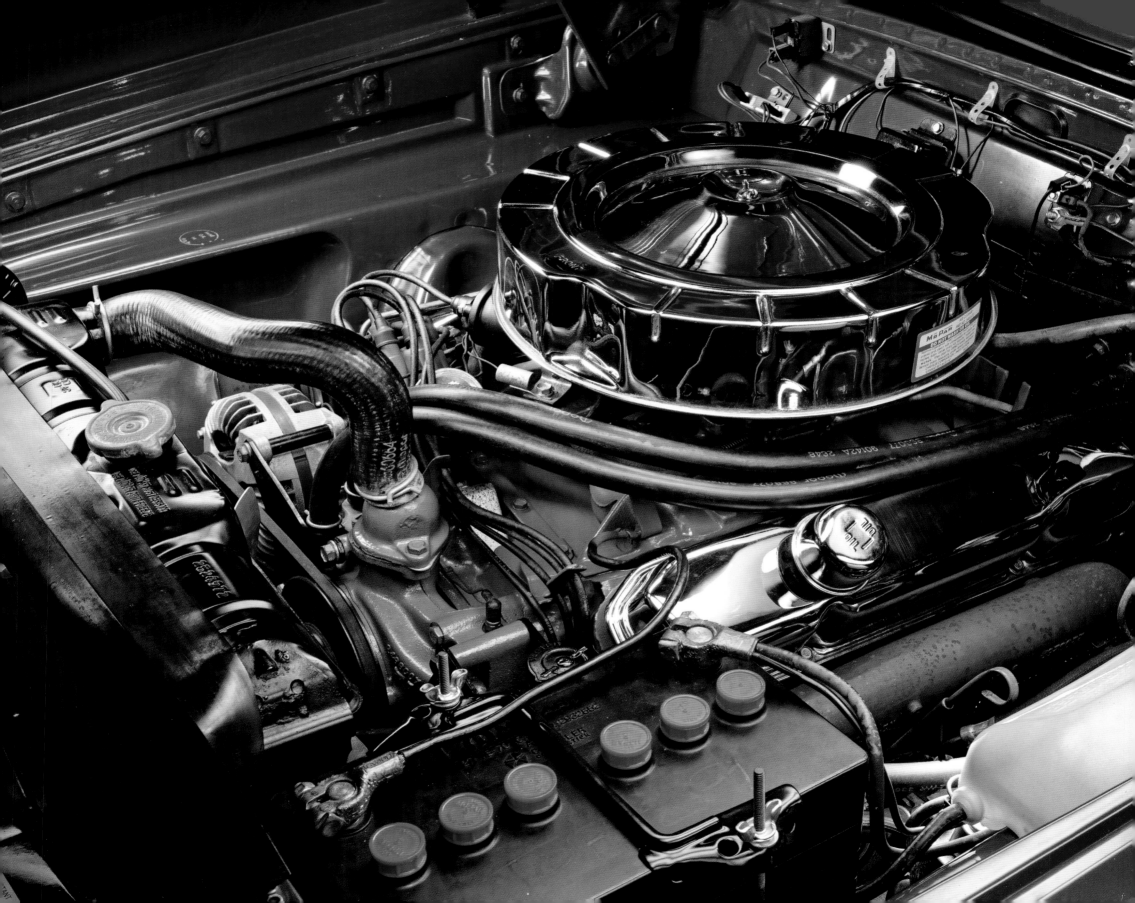

Continued from page 21

seats and a console with space-age detailing. The base engine was the 273, but the 383 was optional. The editors of *Car Life* magazine put a 383 Satellite through its paces and called the engine "a dependable source of stimulation and enjoyment." They praised the interior, saying, "the Satellite seemed a plushy package indeed to be a member of Plymouth's Belvedere line. The standard fold-forward bucket seats are firm and comfortable." They also praised the Satellites clean, crisp styling: "The exterior appearance is also pleasing, continuing Plymouth's adoption of simplicity of line and balanced mass. . . (T)he car is refreshingly free of stylist's blight and highlight-itis."

But the optional Commando 426 Wedge was the powerplant to have, rated at 365 horsepower with 470 lb-ft of torque. No, it wasn't the 426 Max Wedge of the past, nor the 426 Hemi that tore up NASCAR in 1964. The Hemi returned in 1965 to dominate many forms of racing, but not NASCAR, which wouldn't allow it to race as there was no street version. But the Hemi was allowed in the competitive USAC stock car circuit, where Norm Nelson's Satellite took the championship. The Commando 426 Wedge was, however, a very good street engine. *Motor Trend* magazine took a nearly identical '65 Coronet 426-S for a spin and observed 0–60

miles per hour in 7.8 seconds and quarter-mile times of 15.4 at 89 miles per hour. By contrast, *Motor Trend* averaged 16.1 at 89 miles per hour in the 335-horsepower '65 GTO, though the 360-horsepower option could push that number down a few points. And for fans of stealth, a Satellite packing Commando 426 power was only announced by the small 426 "frog leg" emblem on the hood.

Even though the 1965 Satellite had the performance to take the "gee" out of GTO, in the showrooms sales of the GTO kept climbing, from 32,405 in '64 to 75,352 in '65. Plymouth sold 25,201 Satellites, including 1,860 convertibles starting at $2,827. Most Satellites were powered by 273 and 383 engines, and just 1,017 had the 426 Wedge, including 65 convertibles. This 1965 Satellite convertible from The Brothers Collection, wrapped in code TT1 Medium Red Metallic paint, represents the best of these cars and was one of just twenty-one 426 Wedge automatics built.

Plymouth's total sales were up 19 percent over 1964. Much of that increase came from the all-new full-size C-body Fury, but the Belvedere and Satellite made important contributions to overall sales too.

Plymouth's Satellite and all of Chrysler Corporation were ready to blast off.

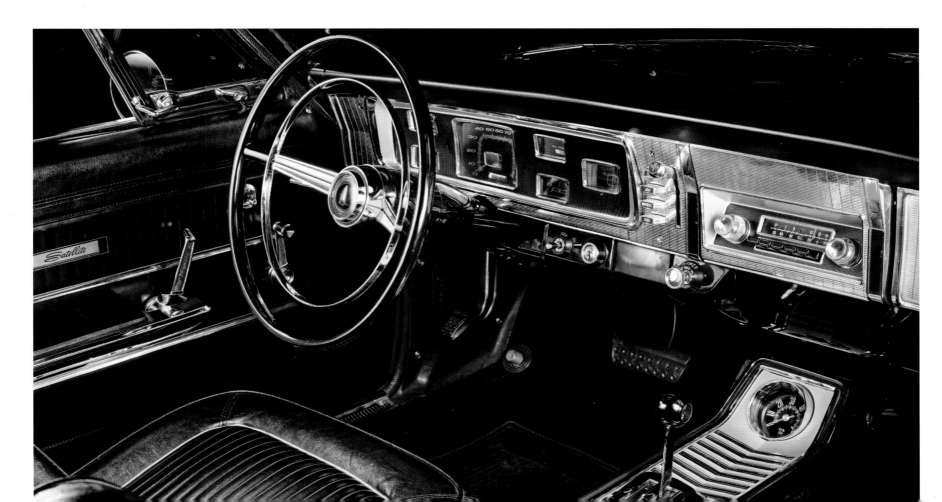

It's one of the hottest, most exciting machines we've tested this season."

—Motor Trend

CHAPTER THREE

1966 DODGE CORONET 426 HEMI

PRODUCTION
96

OPTIONS

E74 426 Hemi ($841.05)

421 AM Transaudio Radio
($57.35)

580 Magnum 500 Wheels
($97.30)

GG1 Dark Green Metallic Paint

H4X Black Vinyl Bench
Seat Interior

HORSEPOWER

425 at 5,000 rpm

TORQUE

490 at 4,000 rpm

"Once free of the garage and onto the highway, there was a temptation to punch it, make the progressive linkage snap back to its last stop, open the rear two barrels of the back Carter 3140 AFB and then all four barrels of the last carb and then all eight barrels of both AFBs. It all happens in a sixtieth of a minute and the TorqueFlite shifts down into low. Everything explodes! There is a frantic sound of huge quantities of air being rammed through eight venturis and the sound of rubber and a shift from First to Second so positive it scares you."

— Eric Dahlquist for *Hot Rod* September 1965.

Your first ride in a 426 Hemi-powered automobile will never be forgotten. But Eric Dahlquist was possibly the first person outside Chrysler to drive a Street Hemi. He took a '65 Coronet engineering mule for a drive at Chrysler's Chelsea Proving Ground way before the rest of the press saw the '66 production car, then tested the showroom version a few months later.

When the 426 Hemi project was launched in 1963, building a street version was not even considered. "Final approval was granted in April 1963," said Tom Hoover, the Chrysler engineer

often called the father of the Hemi. "That hinged, as I recall, on a meeting of the executive committee made up of a number of vice presidents and so forth. I think the committee was chaired by Lynn Townsend, president of the company. Word came down that we should recommend a program that would allow our cars to win the 1964 Daytona 500." That was engineering project A864, and in its first race, Plymouths and Dodges finished the '64 Daytona 500 1-2-3-5. Then Richard Petty earned the NASCAR championship that year.

The key, of course, was the cylinder heads with hemispherical combustion chambers. It wasn't a new idea. The 1911 Peugeot Grand Prix racer had them, and Chrysler's first-generation Hemi used them, so to speed development that concept was adopted to the modern RB engine. The design allowed superior volumetric efficiency and huge valves. How huge? The 2.25-inch intake valves could inhale a pack of cigarettes. The Hemi was costly and complex due to the two rows of rocker arms the combustion chamber design required. It was worth every penny.

In 1965, another Race Hemi, the A865, was offered with twin four-barrels on a cross-ram manifold for drag racing. "Once you got a NASCAR engine, it was relatively simple to make a drag version," Hoover said. The result? At the Winternationals that year, all eleven competitors in Top Stock Eliminator were Hemi Mopars. It was a prescient development—NASCAR's czar Bill France banned the Hemi that year. That edict resulted in the A102 Street Hemi in 1966.

The Street Hemi was wrapped around a very upgraded B-body platform. Lynn Townsend gave Engineering a $57 million budget to turn the B-body into a true midsized automobile, trimming inches from both length and width. As in 1965, Dodge and Plymouth shared common doors and roof, and in an internal competition between the studios, Milt Antonick of the Plymouth

Continued on page 34

"Everything explodes! There is a frantic sound of huge quantities of air being rammed through eight venturis and the sound of rubber and a shift from First to Second so positive it scares you."

– Motor Trend

Continued from page 31

Studio had the winning design, which he said "came together in about a week." Bill Brownlie and his team at the Dodge Studio then went to work creating the hood, trunk, front and rear fenders, and brightwork that made it uniquely a Coronet.

One of the new Hemi Coronets to roll out of the Hamtramck plant was purchased by Tom Hoover himself, a code G Dark Green Coronet 440 with TorqueFlite (440 was the model, not the engine). "The price—$3,285," Tom said. "I ran it 9,000 miles with the original engine. In the meantime, I was building the good engine at the Ramchargers shop. The original engine became the first supercharged Hemi for the Ramchargers Funny Car." Hoover's "good" engine packed aluminum A990 heads, Hooker headers into full-length pipes, and a Racer Brown cam. That Coronet was Hoover's daily driver, winter and summer, for a number of years, a personal engineering exercise that influenced Mopar muscle machines in the future. It was also the fastest car on Interstate 696, the most coveted notoriety in Motor City street racing. That lasted until 1970, when another, faster Hemi Plymouth came along to capture that informal honor.

What would it be like to experience a brand new Hemi Coronet in 1966, just like the one Tom Hoover bought? The Hemi Coronet 440 in The Brothers Collection is about the closest thing to a time machine you can get—it has just 47,281 miles on the odometer and is all original, including the Dark Green paint.

Unforgettable!

Rebel Rouser

Face it. There's a bit of rebel in each of us. Balking at the battle of the budget. Ready to kick the dull driving habit. Fed up on cars with tired blood. Rise up and let the rebel in you dig that tempting new beauty above. 1966 Dodge Coronet 500. Aimed right at your adrenaline glands. Its swingin' styling gift-wraps performance that runs from *pow* to *wow!* Four hot V8s—from standard 273-incher to optional 4-barrel 383-inch growler—supply the go. Inside, strictly show. Take a look at those contour-comfort bucket seats. Standard. Like deep pile carpeting, padded dash and long center console. (Not to mention an optional new tach that swivels for easy eyeballing.) Shows you some class? Part of the plot, man. The beautiful Coronet 500 plot: to move you first-cabin at tourist rates. Investigate it. We don't think you can find a car with Coronet-type action, looks and all-round pizzaz for Coronet's price. So c'mon, reb. Join the drive on Dullsville. Drive a '66 Dodge Coronet.

'66 Dodge Coronet

JOIN THE DODGE REBELLION

DODGE DIVISION — CHRYSLER MOTORS CORPORATION

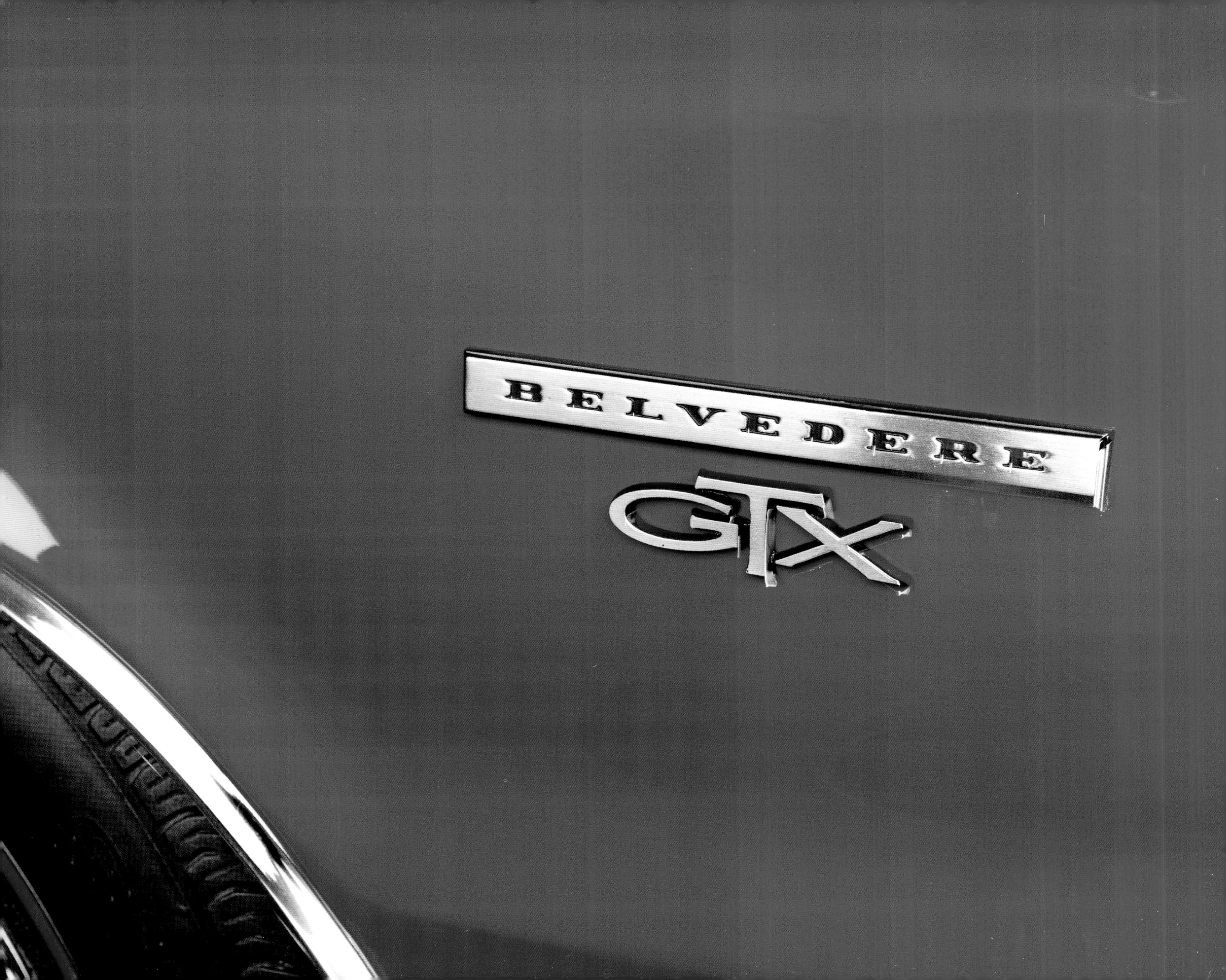
BELVEDERE
GTX

CHAPTER FOUR

1967 PLYMOUTH SATELLITE GTX CONVERTIBLE 426 HEMI

PRODUCTION

10

OPTIONS

73 426 Hemi ($564.00)

421 AM Transaudio Radio ($57.30)

451 Power Brakes ($41.75)

456 Power Steering ($89.65)

580 Magnum 500 Wheels ($97.30)

PP1 Bright Red Paint

P6X Black Vinyl Interior

301 Black Convertible Top

HORSEPOWER

425 at 5,000 rpm

TORQUE

490 at 4,000 rpm

"Plymouth is out to win you over with Belvedere GTX," the magazine ad proclaimed. Plymouth's Product Planning Manager Jack Smith wanted a better competitor to Pontiac's GTO. He played with three letter combinations, then went to Plymouth's head of design, Dick Macadam. Milt Antonick was primarily responsible for the major update of the Belvedere in 1966, and again he crafted the updates for '67.

But for Smith's new car, the Plymouth Studio removed most of the trim from the sporty Satellite, leaving a clean, lean machine. "Because of a minimum of exterior decorations," wrote *Car Life* magazine, "an aggressive, compactly muscular image emerges. This aspect is heightened by the view from the driver's bucket seat: Looking down that broad hood, between the window-dressing 'scoops' and over the pointed, vertical hood ornament, the driver feels sharply inspired with the brute masculinity of the vehicles."

This brute was the GTX starting at $3,178, around $250 more than a GTO. It may have cost more than a GTO, but the GTX came loaded with something a GTO owner could only dream of, the A134 375-horsepower Super Commando 440. What differentiated the Super Commando from the already fine Commando 440 was better flowing heads and a more aggressive hydraulic cam. *Car Craft* called the Super Commando "a street engine with racing ability without the problems of a finely tuned racing mill." That "racing mill" would be the Hemi, of course, a $564 option on the GTX. Their point was not a slap against the Hemi, but for around town driving the 440 GTX was as good, if not better, than the monster 426 "Elephant." Car Life saw 0–60 miles per hour in 6.6 seconds testing the '67 GTX. But really, better than the Hemi? In 1968 *Car Life* got the answer by pitting matching 440s and Hemi GTXs on the strip. Off the line, the 440 was faster, but by the 400-foot mark the Hemi drew even. Then the Hemi's huge pack-of-Marlboro-sucking intake ports started coming into their own, and it was gone. One other bonus of the 440 was it came with Chrysler's five-year/50,000-mile warranty, while the Hemi was only twelve years/12,000 miles.

Continued on page 40

The only chance you'll get to pass Richard Petty's Hemi!

Small wonder, what with its high-performance 426-cubic-inch hemispherical-head V-8. Plymouth Belvedere . . . a beautiful piece of hairy machinery! Everything about the Hemi package is designed to move you out, fast. Like four-barrel carbs. Dual-breaker distributor. High-lift, high-overlap cam. Special plugs, pistons and double valve springs. Low-back-pressure, dual-exhaust system. Special Blue Streak tires. Wide-base, Safety-Rim wheels. Oversize front torsion bars. Sway bar.

Added-leaf, high-rate rear springs. And heavy-duty shocks. For performance stops, optional front-wheel disc brakes. Now that we've told you what goes into making a Hemi-powered Plymouth such a great winner, we'll tell you what it takes to beat one. Another Hemi-powered Plymouth.

PLYMOUTH DIVISION  **CHRYSLER** MOTORS CORPORATION

Continued from page 37

So it's easy to see why 12,010 GTXs were sold in 1967, but also why just 733 were Hemi powered. The Hemi maybe wasn't as necessary for performance as it was before the Super Commando 440 came along, but make no mistake: it was still King. Another "King" was making that point: Richard Petty. Throughout 1967, Petty was marching to his second NASCAR Grand National championship in a season never to be equaled—twenty-seven victories out of forty-nine races. At one point King Richard won ten races in a row. This was before the modern era of NASCAR, and Petty captured victories on dirt tracks, short ovals, and speedways. "What makes Richard run?" *Car Life* took a close look at this legendary race car and concluded: "A chassis that can take the torture of Daytona and a surprisingly stock Hemi." This was not some tube-framed purpose-built race car with not one production part—like today's stock cars. No, this was a Plymouth that Richard Petty personally picked up at the St. Louis assembly plant before building it into the winningest NASCAR stock car in history.

Another GTX from down South was also tearing up the drag strips of the nation. Ronnie Sox and Buddy Martin had been competitors until Martin realized

"Ronnie's skills as a driver were a gift," he told National Dragster in 2001. "He was very coordinated with the hand and foot. In addition to his shifting, his reaction times were outstanding." They switched from Mercury to Plymouth in 1965, and in '67 campaigned a 340 Barracuda and 440 and Hemi GTXs in Stock and Super Stock classes. Their GTX won major events at Bristol in 1967 and the 1968 Springnationals at Englishtown, along with countless other races. They also gave clinics at dealerships all over the nation to show other Plymouth owners how to race at the strip.

Along with the GTX hardtop and coupe, a convertible was available starting at $3,418. These are rare brutes, since just 686 ragtops were ordered, and just 17 had Hemi power, 10 with the TorqueFlite automatic. The Brothers Collection is home to possibly the nicest of those convertibles, clothed in code PP1 Bright Red paint. There are just over 20,000 miles on it too, making you wonder how anyone could resist the urge to drive it.

Like the Plymouth ad said, the only way to pass Richard Petty's GTX—or *any* GTX—is if it's on a trailer.

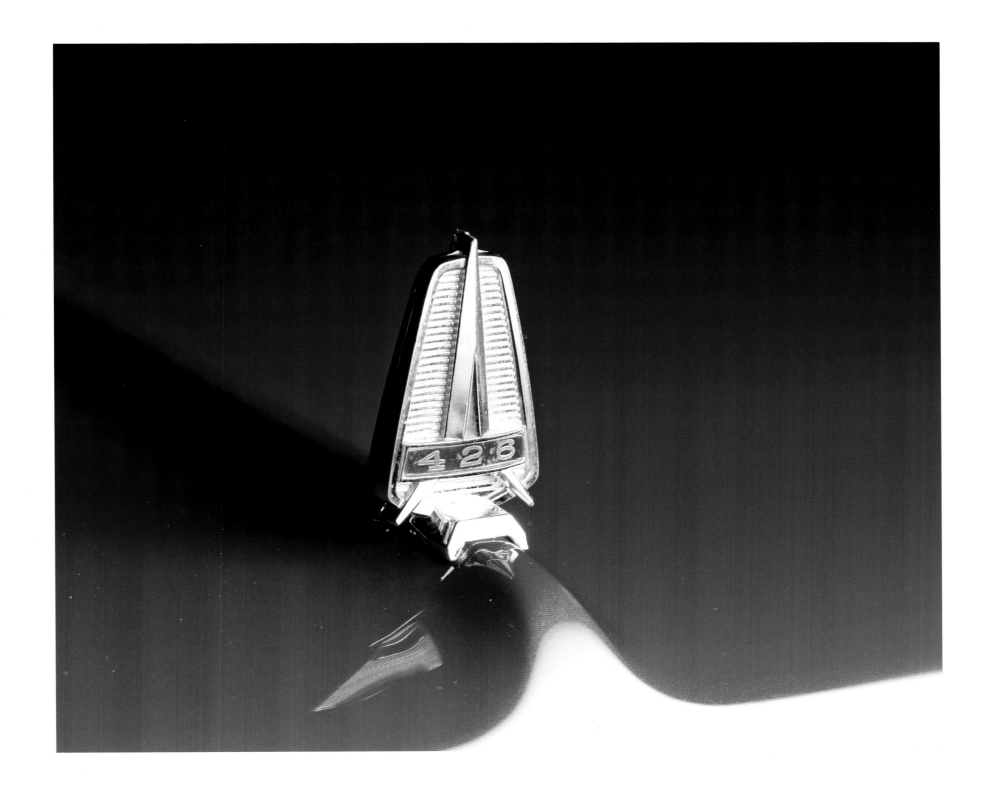

country, but it is not as 'rough' as the Chevy engine. It is extremely docile the engine show its competition heritage and performance potential."

—Road Test

CHAPTER FIVE

1967 DODGE CHARGER 426 HEMI

PRODUCTION
58

OPTIONS

456 Power Steering ($89.65)

484 Electric Clock ($15.30)

458 Power Windows
($100.25)

483 Bumper Guards ($30.85)

WW1 White Paint

PBX Black Vinyl Interior

HORSEPOWER

425 at 5,000 rpm

TORQUE

490 AT 4,000 rpm

There's an adage in Detroit: You can sell an old man a young man's car, but you can never sell a young man an old man's car. And in 1966, Dodge was perceived as selling old man's cars.

The reality was that the average Dodge buyer in 1966 was fifty years old, while the median age of the US population, thanks to the Baby Boom, was twenty. The "Dodge Revolution" advertising campaign that year, with pretty Pam Austin as spokeswoman, started to change perceptions. But on January 1, 1966, a two-ton image maker was announced: Dodge Charger.

As with most things in Detroit, the genesis of the Charger took place three years before its introduction. Designer Carl "Cam" Cameron created a series of renderings of a car he called "Monte Carlo." This was years before a Chevrolet of the same name was introduced, and Cameron was playing off the name of Dodge's

future full-sized car, the Monaco. Cameron gave his concept a long fastback roofline, perhaps to echo the Plymouth Barracuda's roof that was being finalized at that time, but the concave rear window design that flowed through the rear deck to the full-width taillights was genuinely unique. Surface treatments along the side and on the hood suggested Dodge's mid-sized Coronet, but taken up a notch, while the disappearing headlights were an elegant touch. Cameron had just created Dodge's vision of the personal luxury car, in the mold of the Ford Thunderbird and Buick Riviera.

Dodge's chief designer, Bill Brownlie, was tasked with turning Carl Cameron's concept into reality. "Money and timing dictated a derivative of an existing product so the first Charger became a fastback derivative of the Coronet two-door hardtop," Bert Bouwkamp, Chief Engineer and Manager of Dodge

Passenger Car Product Planning, recalled. "Considering the limitations of relatively short Coronet front sheet metal and long 'B' body rear overhang, Bill Brownlie and his team did an exceptional job in designing this vehicle."

Under Cameron's slick body was an interior keeping with the personal luxury theme. The Charger featured four bucket seats, and the console ran the entire length of the interior. The rear buckets folded down, leaving a huge expanse of storage under the large, sloping rear window. The unique instrument panel glowed at night with electroluminescent gauges. Comfortable, functional, yet like something out of *The Jetson's*, the Charger's interior was a futuristic command module.

Powering the Charger was typical Coronet power: 318 standard, 383 and Hemi optional. The 440 Magnum was added in 1967. While not the runaway hit of Ford's Mustang, the sleek Charger sold well nonetheless. a total of 37,344 Chargers had been built in the abbreviated '66 model year, and the press gave it generally glowing reviews, with *High Performance CARS* magazine giving the Charger its annual Top Performance Car of the Year award.

The Charger had been successful on the race track, too. David Pearson drove Cotton Owens's #6 Charger and Coronet to the NASCAR championship in 1966, using the Coronet for fourteen of his fifteen wins, while the aerodynamic Charger was favored for faster tracks. The Charger proved to be fast, but unstable, at high speed. The fastback roof was causing "lift" at the rear as speed increased. Testing revealed all that was needed was a small spoiler on the tail to cure the lift, but NASCAR dictated factory parts only. Dodge built 85 Chargers in '66 with the spoiler to satisfy NASCAR's demands, and all Hemi Chargers for '67 were so equipped.

Since Chargers had only been built for the last six months of the '66 model year, it rolled into 1967 with few changes. Fender-mounted turn signal indicators were now standard, the interior console that ran the entire length of the interior in '66 was now a normal length, and a "mother-in-law" center rear seat was a no-cost option.

A beautiful white Hemi Charger was displayed at the 1967 Toronto International Auto Show. When built, the car was detailed for the show circuit, including chassis components painted gloss black, to look smashing up on its platform. It was also heavily optioned, with bumper guards, power steering and windows, and electric clock. The 426 Hemi is backed by the proven A727 TorqueFlite 3-speed automatic. Oddly the three-piece rear NASCAR spoiler was installed facing backward. After the show it was sold by Robin Dodge in Picton, Ontario, to H. J. McFarland. The Charger remained in Canada until recent years, one of only two '67 Hemi Chargers sold there. It now resides in The Brothers Collection.

Continued on page 51

Continued from page 46

For all the promise of the first Dodge Charger, 1967 would prove to be a bitter disappointment. Just 15,788 were sold, including 177 Hemi-powered Chargers (58 with TorqueFlite). In NASCAR, '66 champ David Pearson returned in Cotton Owens's Chargers, but only won two races early in the season before Richard Petty's Plymouth began its rewriting of the record books.

It's quite ironic that David Pearson defected to Ford in 1968. The car he drove to his second NASCAR championship in '68, and his third in '69, was a spankin' new Ford Torino, prepped by the factory Holman-Moody team. That all-new Torino sure looked like a total ripoff of the 1966–1967 Charger's fastback design. It even included a built-in rear spoiler. Sales of the Torino in 1968 and 1969 were good too—74,135 and 17,951 units, respectively. They say imitation is the sincerest form of flattery, right? Or could it be the 1966–1967 Dodge Charger was just a little too far ahead of its time?

"With barely enough miles on the clock to permit high-speed strip at Carlsbad. E.T.s ran in the mid-14-second bracket in a genuine, unprepared street machine without benefit

driving, we turned the Hemi-Charger loose on the drag and our best trap speed was 100.33. All of this was of cheater slicks."

—*Motor Trend*

CHAPTER SIX

1967 DODGE CORONET R/T 426 HEMI

PRODUCTION

162

OPTIONS

74 426 Hemi ($564.00)

486 Console ($52.85)

577 Tachometer ($48.70)

458 Power Windows ($100.25)

458 Power Steering ($89.65)

451 Power Brakes ($41.75)

580 Road Wheels ($97.30)

PP1 Bright Red Paint

P6X Black Vinyl Interior

HORSEPOWER

425 at 5,000 rpm

TORQUE

490 at 4,000 rpm

It must have been a difficult decision for some Dodge buyers in 1967: Charger or Coronet R/T? The lines blurred much more than the previous year. Much of the sleek sheet metal that Carl Cameron crafted for the '66 Charger now was featured on the '67 Coronet. Even the grille on the Coronet R/T now looked like the Charger's with the headlights exposed. Of course, the Charger had that cool fastback roof and space-age interior, while Coronet R/T had the stylish hardtop and convertible options. Plus, both shared the same powertrains, the incredible 426 Hemi and the new 440 Magnum, though the Charger could be ordered with smaller engines. It came down to the kind of money you'd have to spend, and the kind of statement you'd want to make—style with performance, or performance with style.

Starting at $3,199, the Coronet R/T was an amazingly complete package. Loads of options could be added, but even without them it was a sharp set of wheels that turned heads and stopped clocks—*Motor Trend* stopped theirs at 0–60 in 7.2 seconds, the quarter in 15.4, with the 440 Magnum on street tires with a passenger in the front seat.

On the track, the Coronet R/T could do amazing things too. "Dandy" Dick Landy set the AHRA B/SA national record in 1967 with a Coronet R/T 440 at 12.61 at 110.02 miles per hour. Those were mostly stock automobiles running headers and slicks (and a little of Landy's legendary tuning magic).

But there was that famous option on the order form, code 74. The 426 Hemi. How did a Coronet R/T 440 compare to the

Hemi costing an additional $564? *Motor Trend*, in their June 1967 issue, settled the score: "Ever since early model year, when we saw the more down-to-earth Magnum consistently whip one of its exotic King Kong Hemi brethren in a series of quarter-mile bashes, we have wondered about the phrase ' . . . performance approaches that of the 426 Hemi . . . ' in Dodge's descriptive literature for the Magnum engine. For this reason we decided to get one of each, identically equipped in all essential respects, and make a mano a mano, to borrow an expression from bullfighting, trial of the two."

On the drag strip, with street tires, *Motor Trend* discovered: "When running together, the Magnum would leap into the lead at the start, and the Hemi would start to close rapidly and catch it at the end—but just after the quarter mark and the end of the race. . . . Also, another thing we came to notice about both cars that added to our enjoyment and which we feel any owner would doubly appreciate: the sheer ruggedness and built-to-last impression we got from testing them. They seemed to thrive on the kind of treatment we gave them. No howls developed in the rear axles: nothing seemed about to break or fall off. In short, they seemed completely unaffected by all the hard running, and they ran better afterwards."

ENTER THE BIG BORE HUNTER

Dodge Coronet R/T... with 440-Magnum

Drag fans, here's your car. Coronet R/T packs 440 cubic inches of go ! The big-inch, deep-breathing 440-Magnum sports a special 4-barrel carburetor, larger exhaust valves, longer duration cam and low-restriction dual exhaust. Underneath there's a heavy-duty

suspension with sway bar and special shock absorbers for better handling, high-performance nylon cord Red Streak tires, and big 3-inch-wide brakes—front and rear—for surer stops. Front disc brakes are optional. An extra leaf in the right rear spring copes with torque and helps prevent

wheel hop. Coronet R/T comes on strong with sizzling style, too. Body side paint stripes, distinctive hood air-scoop design, bucket front seats, and special R/T insignia put it lengths ahead of the look-alike crowd. Hunting for trophy-winning performance that handles

beautifully on the road ? Check the odds. They're 440 to 1 in favor of Coronet R/T . . . a balanced automobile engineered for the enthusiast.

"Dodge Rebellion Operation '67 Wants You"

Dodge

R/T stood for "road and track," and *Motor Trend* discovered both cars lived up to the name: "We've emphasized the straight-line performance of these cars because it is the most spectacular. But both come with good suspensions and brakes and hence make very good road cars, too."

Road Test magazine called the Coronet R/T "the top muscle car in 1967," and when you look at its comparably priced competition, they might be right. Other than the R/T's cousin, the Plymouth GTX, everyone had much smaller engines at the top of their regular options, from the Ford and Mercury's 390, to Chevrolet's 396, to the 400-cubic-inch engines powering

the GTO, Olds 442, and Buick GS. Bargain performance in a stylish package is what the Coronet R/T was all about, and 10,181 were sold, including 628 convertibles.

But some buyers just didn't want a bargain. They wanted nothing but the best a Coronet R/T could give them. Order the $3,199 R/T, and dress it in code PP1 Bright Red paint. Add the console, tach, and power windows, steering, and brakes. Then top it off with the 426 Hemi with the slick-shifting TorqueFlite automatic and the beautiful Kelsey-Hayes Magnum 500 road wheels. That's one expensive Coronet R/T. Maybe *this* is the real leader of the Dodge Rebellion?

"We've emphasized the straight-line performance
But both come with good suspensions and

of these cars because it is the most spectacular.
brakes and hence make very good road cars, too."

—*Motor Trend*

PART 2

FLAT

Chrysler was doing something right. In 1961, Chrysler Corporation had just 9.7 percent of the US market share, according to the trade publication *Ward's Auto World*. Its popular Plymouth division had its lowest sales since 1935, and 1935 was right in the midst of the Great Depression. Chrysler was on the ropes in 1961, and it didn't look good.

In just six years, what a change. By the end of the 1967 model year, Chrysler was now at 15.2 percent market share, while Ford was down 2.9 percent and GM down 1.8 percent. More important, Dodge and Plymouth were capturing the youth market just as that demographic was reaching the age they could buy cars. The Dodge Rebellion advertising campaign, with Pam Austin as the face of the brand, was identified by 87 percent of consumers as promoting the Dodge brand. The Scholastic Research Center asked male students ages fifteen to eighteen "which car advertising appeals most to you this year?" The answer was Dodge.

For 1968 Dodge would begin the Dodge Fever advertising promotion with gorgeous yet down-to-earth Joan Anita Parker. Plymouth would "win you over" as "the beat goes on" with music by Petula Clark. Most importantly, new performance machines would also be in the showrooms for '68. It was going to get real interesting, real fast.

OUT

CHAPTER SEVEN

1968 DODGE CHARGER 426 HEMI

PRODUCTION

211

OPTIONS

73 426 Hemi ($604.75)

393 Manual 4-Speed
Transmission ($188.05)

458 Power Windows
($100.25)

LL1 Medium Turquoise
Metallic Paint

C6X Black Vinyl Interior

HORSEPOWER

425 at 5,000 rpm

TORQUE

490 at 4,000 rpm

Fashion designer and automobile collector Ralph Lauren said it well: "I don't design clothes. I design dreams." Could it have been a similar philosophy at work in the Dodge Studio when it created the timeless 1968 Dodge Charger?

When *Car and Driver* tested the '68 Charger, they remarked, "It looks like the Chrysler Corporation is flat out in the automobile business again. The only 1968 car which comes close to challenging the new Charger for styling accolades is the new Corvette, which is remarkably similar to the Charger, particularly when viewed from the rear quarter . . . Originality takes guts in Dodge's position as the smaller division of the number three automaker, but the Charger's aerodynamic wedge theme is not only distinctly new but it is very like the new breed of wind-tunnel tested sports/racing cars which are just now making their debut in the 1967 Can-Am series."

Diran Yazejian, a young designer at the time, told allpar. com: "Bill Brownlie, Dodge Studio Executive Designer, wanted

an evolutionary design from the '66—a fastback. Meanwhile, off in a corner of the Dodge Studio, Richard Sias was making a 1/10 scale 'speed form' clay model. It was 'aircrafty' and had the double-diamond shapes built into its form, but it wasn't a fastback. . . . The 'sail panels' made it look fastback enough to satisfy Brownlie.

"It was such an exciting shape that Chuck Mitchell, Chief Designer, wondered if it could be morphed into a B-body size car," Yazejian continued. "Since the program hadn't yet started, a full-size clay model was started while hidden behind two 20-foot blackboards. Frank Ruff, B-body Car Line Manager, with his experience and Richard Sias' vision, directed the clay modelers to what soon looked like the '68 Charger. Everybody knew it was a winner. While still behind the boards, it was informally shown to Bob McCurry, Dodge Division VP. He approved it on the spot; it was moved out onto a regular platform in the studio, finalized, and refined, and released to

Join the fun. Catch
DODGE fever

customer
care

Dodge   CHRYSLER
MOTORS CORPORATION

Engineering." Having the approval of Elwood Engle was also a big boost, as he proclaimed, "Now, *that's* what a car should look like."

Detroit design studios just didn't work this way. There were always studio design competitions for new models, then management reviews, consumer clinics, more management reviews, and other formalities before a design was chosen. Not the second-generation Charger. It looked *so* right that Dodge's leadership pulled the trigger immediately.

Everything underneath the shapely skin was standard B-body Coronet, reducing cost and making the transition from concept to showroom easier. Only the windshield and A-pillars were shared with the other B-body cars. Powertrain also matched the Coronet. The base Charger model had the 318 V-8

as standard, so the performance R/T model with its standard 440 Magnum (and optional Hemi) was the one to buy. Graphic designer Harvey Winn adopted his bumblebee stripe from the Coronet R/T, but if that was too showy for a buyer, it could be deleted. "With all this performance image going for the Charger," said *Car and Driver*, "we just had to order an engine to go with it—and when you're talking a Chrysler product, the performance engine is the Hemi. There just isn't more honest horsepower available off the showroom floor than you get from this bright orange monster." Honest, as in 0–60 in 4.8 seconds, and the quarter-mile in 13.5 at 105 miles per hour. Note, this was in a Charger packed with test equipment weighing in at 4,346 pounds.

Dodge production planners, using sales of the 1966–1967 Charger as a baseline, estimated 20,000 '68 Chargers would be sold. But the new Dodge

Fever ad campaign had gone viral, and by the end of the model year, 92,590 Chargers were sold, including 475 with Hemis. Demand was so high that Hamtramck Assembly couldn't keep up, and the St. Louis plant also began building Chargers.

As beautiful as all second-generation Chargers are, The Brothers Collection is home to an R/T that is really unique. The '68 is Hemi-powered, of course, with four-speed, one of 211 so equipped. The R/T stripe was deleted, as was the console, and since air conditioning was not available with the Hemi, it has the optional power windows. What's more, the code LL1 Medium Turquoise Metallic Paint is rarely seen, and it is believed this is the *only* '68 Hemi Charger in this color.

Maybe this is what dreaming in color looks like.

"It looks like the Chrysler Corporation is flat out in the which comes close to challenging the new Charger

automobile business again. The only 1968 car for styling accolades is the new Corvette . . . "

—Car and Driver

CHAPTER EIGHT

1968 PLYMOUTH ROAD RUNNER HEMI

PRODUCTION
61

OPTIONS

74 426 Hemi ($714.30)

395 TorqueFlite ($38.95)

508 Performance Hood Paint Treatment ($17.55)

WW1 Alpine White Paint

HORSEPOWER

425 at 5,000 rpm

TORQUE

490 at 4,000 rpm

It just didn't seem right. The very demographic targeted by the muscle car—young men in their late teens or early twenties—often could not afford the very cars they lusted after. A base Pontiac GTO cost $3,101 in 1968; add the 360-horsepower Ram Air engine and a few options (and you always add a few options, right?) and the price could cross the $3,750 mark. But the average income in '68 was $5,571.76, and you can bet someone right out of high school, or young veterans returning from Vietnam, didn't make that kind of money.

Jack Smith was manager of the midsized Plymouth product planning group. In a 2000 talk, Smith recalled his idea: "It had to please the kids if it was going to be successful. Number One, it had to do 0 to 60 in under seven seconds, right off the showroom floor . . . It was to be stock, but it had to do over 100 miles per hour in the quarter-mile in less than fifteen seconds.

That was another objective. Yet another objective was that it had to have, as standard equipment, all the mechanical toys the kids wanted: high-performance brakes, transmission, and stuff like that. Lastly, it had to sell for under $3,000." It was a brilliant idea, but it was only weeks before the 1968 cars would be in the showrooms.

Most of the pieces were already in place, including a nice restyle of the Plymouth Belvedere. Plymouth engineers then started with the Belvedere I Coupe, Plymouth's basic family/fleet midsize. Only a basic bench-seat interior was offered, with no console and no carpeting, just rubber mats. By reaching into the police car parts bins (Chrysler had 51 percent of the police market), the new car had heavy-duty brakes, suspension, and rear axle. Chrysler's trusty 383-cubic-inch V-8 would power it, but with the 440 GTX cam and heads

added, creating the new 383 Magnum exclusive to this car. Three hundred thirty-five horsepower may not seem like much, but in this 3,200-pound projectile it could humiliate cars with much more grunt. If this wasn't fast enough, the legendary 426 Street Hemi was the only engine option, at a hefty $714. At $2,896 for the post coupe, $3,034 for the hardtop, it had potential and Plymouth planned on selling maybe 2,500 that year.

Now Jack Smith had to make it memorable. Chrysler's ad agency, Young & Rubicam, put their best creatives on the task of selecting a name for the new youth-oriented car. They suggested Lamancha. Nice try. Thankfully, Smith's assistant had a better suggestion: "Those of you who have seen the cartoons know that Wile E. Coyote is always trying to snag Road Runner, and Road Runner cannot be caught," Smith recounted the assistant saying. "He cannot be caught because he is so agile. . . . He can take off the line very quickly! When he gets going, he is very fast. Now, anything that goes that fast has to be able to stop very quickly; stop on a dime. You can see the characteristics that he had . . . And best of all, he whoops: Beep, beep!"

A licensing agreement with Warner Brothers Studio for the use of the cartoon character was quickly arranged (it cost Chrysler $50,000), and the Plymouth Road Runner was born. In a final stroke of genius, the Spartan Horn Company took an item they made for the military, drove the cost down to $0.47 above a stock piece, and the famous Road Runner horn was born. Jack Smith remembered that the only new component necessary was the mounting bracket, which cost $243 to tool.

The Road Runner was unquestionably the surprise hit of 1968, with 44,948 cars sold, 29,240 coupes, 15,358 hardtops. *Car Life* magazine recorded 0–60 in 7.3 seconds and 15.37 at 91.4 in the quarter with a 383 and a load of test equipment. Most Road Runner buyers couldn't afford the Hemi, which would be like a $7,000 option today, but 840

Road Runner Coupe

BEEP-BEEP!

1968

Road Runner

**Brilliant performance.
And the price is right. Road Runner
is what "out of sight" is all about.**

Get this. Road Runner's got a standard engine so exclusive you can't even get it on another Plymouth. It's called the Road Runner 383. Has a 4-barrel carb. All this and more in a new 2-door coupe that's exclusive among Plymouth's competition. (By giving it the same roof as our hardtops, you get frameless front door glass. And the rear windows tip out.)

For kicks, you get a Road Runner nameplate on the dash and deck lid. Another on the doors. Plus a cartoon Road Runner on the deck lid, the doors and on the instrument panel

The Plymouth win-you-over beat goes on.

coupes and 169 hardtops were ordered. How fun was that? *Car and Driver* saw a tire-melting 13.54 at 105 in their 1,320-foot trips!

The '68 Hemi Road Runner hardtop in The Brothers Collection represents one of the great performance machines of all time. It's mostly original, with a respray over thirty years old and a recovered bench seat. Just sixty-one Hemi hardtops were ordered with the column-shifted A727 TorqueFlite, so this is one rare bird.

The Pontiac GTO may have been *Motor Trend* Car of the Year in 1968, but on the street even the Ram Air GTO was more like Wile E. Coyote—0–60 in 6.6, the quarter in 14.53 at 99.7 according to *Car Life*.

As a Plymouth ad that year stated: "Road Runner is what 'out of sight' is all about."

"To say the Road Runner scored heavily in the performance part
It was the quickest in acceleration, stopped in the shortest distance

of the test is Anglo Saxon understatement in the best tradition.
and ranked second in handling. That is a pretty tough record."

—*Car and Driver*

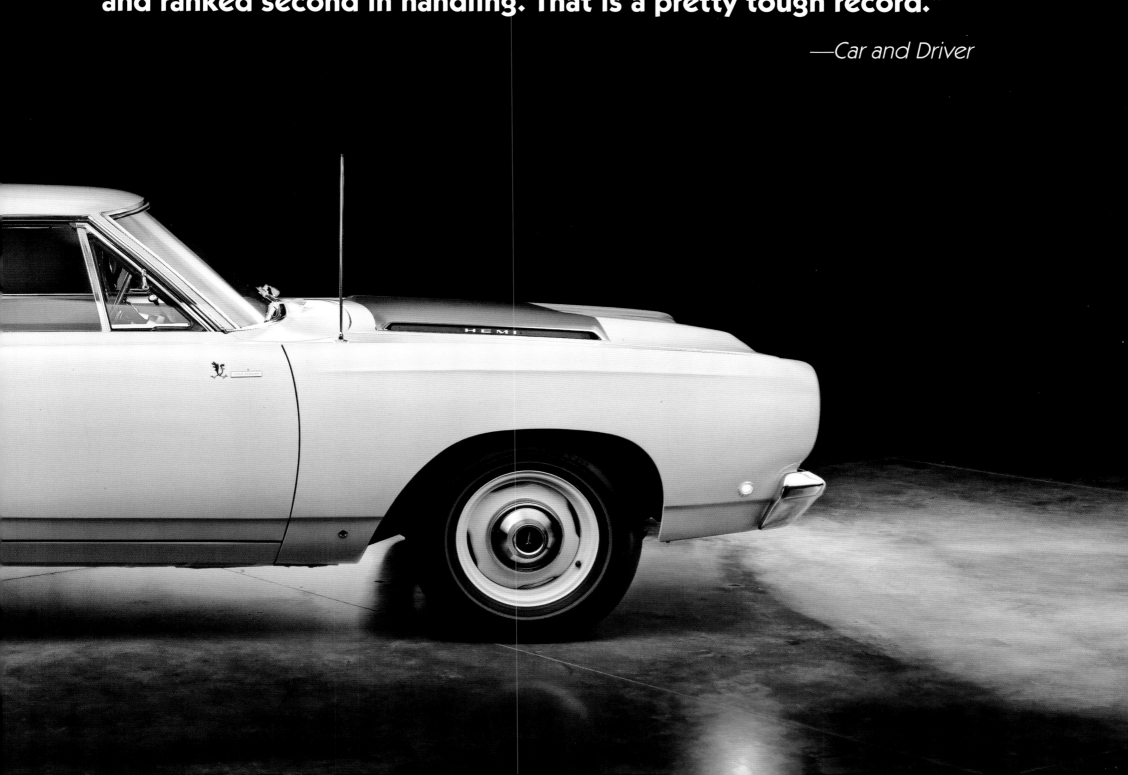

PRODUCTION

1,412

OPTIONS

A12 440 6-BBL Engine
Package ($462.80)

N85 Tachometer ($50.15)

HORSEPOWER

390 at 4,700 rpm

TORQUE

490 at 3,600 rpm

1969 PLYMOUTH ROAD RUNNER 440 6-BARREL A12

After the success of the '68 Road Runner, it was named *Motor Trend* Car of the Year for 1969. The Brothers Collection features a number of '69 'Runners, but something about this one is, well, different. There is practically nothing extraneous, just basic painted steel wheels and redline tires, a matte-black fiberglass hood with a large functional scoop, and a basic black bench seat interior. The only adornment is the "440 6BBL" sticker on the hood scoop, the small cartoon birds, and the bright High Impact Paint color. In a world of wannabe performance machines with their bold stripes, fake scoops, and useless spoilers, the A12 Road Runners are like an Olympic sprinter—nothing but lean, mean muscle.

When the first A12 Road Runner rolled off the Lynch Road assembly line on March 11, 1969, the press didn't know what this car was about. Then on March 30 *Super Stock* magazine was handed the keys to that same Performance Red A12 at Cecil County Dragway in Delaware, and they soon found out. The editors, Jim McCraw and Ro McGonegal, were able to storm the quarter-mile at a stunning 13.24 at 110.70 miles per hour. Then the legendary Ronnie Sox showed up at the track. In ten runs, "Mr. 4-Speed" averaged 13.14 at 110.85.

"In three runs Sox was able go 12.98-111.52, 12.92-111.66, 12.91-111.80," reported *Super Stock*. "In order to get into the twelves, nothing more was necessary than to remove the air cleaner element." And the NHRA was there to verify the A12 was indeed factory stock.

What lurked beneath that lift-off hood was not a legendary Hemi, but a 440 Magnum six-barrel. A number of cars in the fifties and sixties offered three deuces (including the original Pontiac GTO), but the A12's were mounted atop Chrysler's powerful 440 Magnum. The intake manifold was an Edelbrock aluminum unit with factory part number. Around town the central 2300-series Holley two-barrel carb did all the work, but stomp the throttle and the outer Holleys kicked in for a total of about 1,200 cfm. Also included was a dual-breaker distributor, special camshaft, heavy-duty valve springs, chrome-flashed valve stems, moly-filled rings, Hemi oil pump, and Magnafluxed connecting rods. Chrysler said the "six-barrel" produced 390 horsepower at 4,700 rpm with 390 lbs-ft of torque at 3,600 rpm, but the NHRA, whose business was maintaining parity in the Stock classes, factored it at 410-horsepower.

1969 "BOSS" MAKES FIRST TIMED RUNS--NHRA MANS THE CLOCKS.

PLYMOUTH TEL LS IT LIKE IT IS.

The A12 performance package didn't stop with the engine. Heavy-duty manual and automatic transmissions were borrowed from the Hemi cars. The only differential offered was the bulletproof Dana 60 Sure-Grip with 4.10:1 gears. Underneath was the Belvedere's S15 Police Handling package. The Hi Impact Paint colors (Performance Red, Bahama Yellow, Rallye Green, and Vitamin C Orange) were standard, but any other Road Runner color could be ordered. If you wanted air conditioning, cruise control, fancy wheels, or a convertible top, you were shopping for the wrong car.

Yet for all this monstrous speed, the A12 was a joy to drive on the street. As *Super Stock* reported: " . . . Our first visit with the car was Interstate

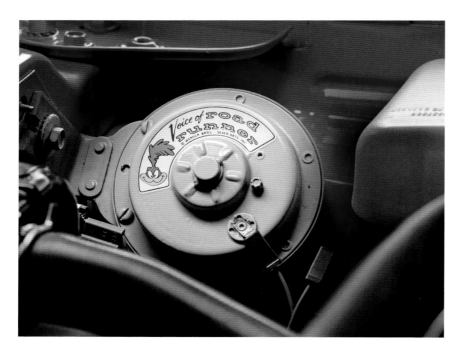

highways at high speeds. We were impressed. The tires made it ride and handle beautifully, and the carbs—well, when they came in at about 4,000 rpm, it was a whole new ball game."

Dodge also built an A12, the 1969 Coronet Super Bee Six-Pack. Only the Lynch Road plant in Detroit built the A12, and Engineering provided a twenty-nine-step instruction list to the line workers detailing how the cars were to be assembled. As amazing as the performance was, when you factor in the price, the A12 was an incredible package. At $462.80, the A12 package was a real deal, and despite its late debut and Spartan nature, 1,412 were built. Clearly, Chrysler spent the money on only the essentials.

After the muscle era ended, a review of the times of all the street machines the factories built revealed a shocking statistic. The fastest cars of the sixties were the 427 Cobra and L88 Corvette, both ultra-rare, ultra-expensive two-seat sports/racing cars. What about real-world vehicles? The A12 Road Runner topped the list. Faster than the Chevys, the Pontiacs, the Fords—even the Street Hemis! Sure, on the racetrack the 426 Hemi, Ford's Boss 429, and Chevy's L88 were at home, but they were too race-focused when detuned for the street. But the 440 six-barrel in the lightweight Road Runner was perfectly optimized for a good street fight.

Whatever happened to that first A12, the one Ronnie Sox set that unbeatable time in? It's in The Brothers Collection. You're looking at it!

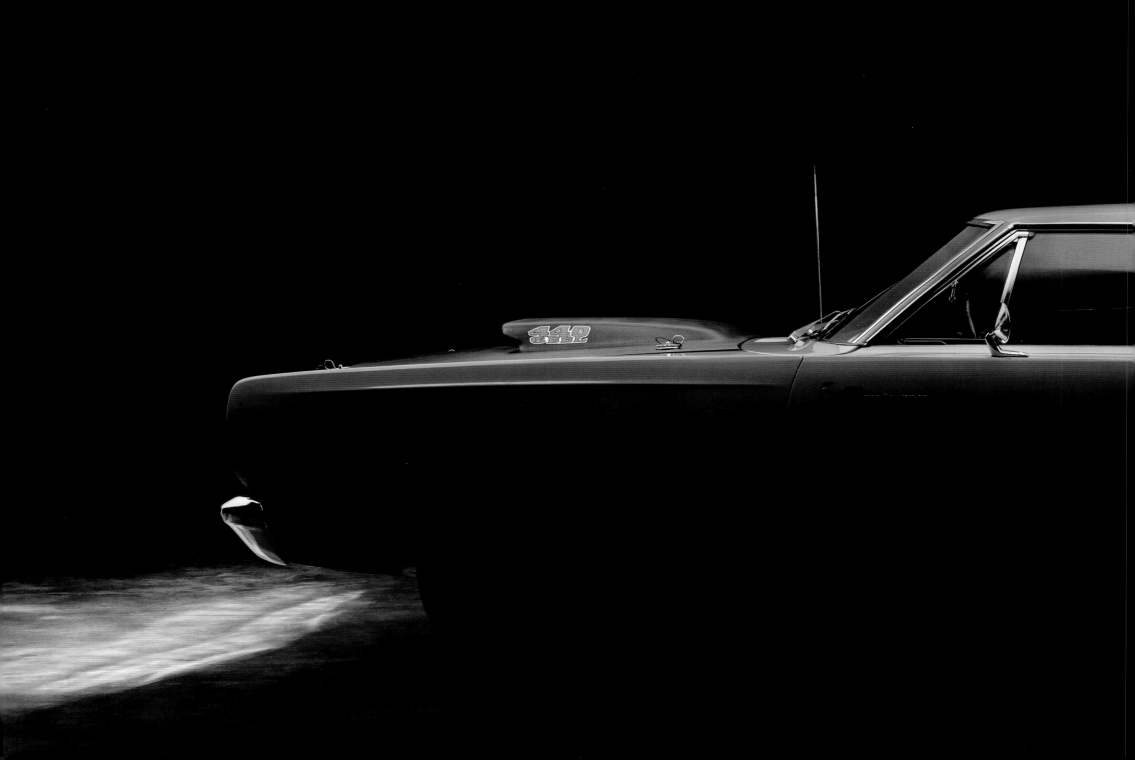

"In three runs Sox was able go 12.98-111.52, nothing more was necessary than to remove

12.92-111.66, 12.91-111.80. In order to get into the twelves, the air cleaner element."

—*Super Stock*

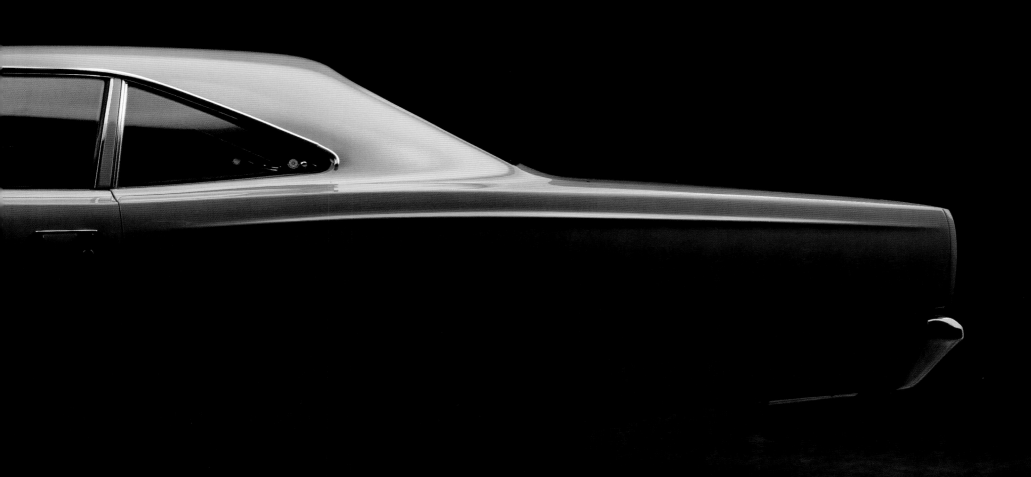

CHAPTER TEN

1969 PLYMOUTH BARRACUDA COUPE MOD TOP

PRODUCTION

937

OPTIONS

Mod Top Vinyl Top ($90)

Mod Top Interior ($40)

Y2 Sunfire Yellow Paint

HORSEPOWER

230 at 4,400 rpm

TORQUE

340 at 2,400 rpm

"It's a sign of the times," sang British pop star Petula Clark in the sixties, and the signs were everywhere. The mod fashions from London's Carnaby Street, the Flower Power peace movement, the hippies from San Francisco's Haight-Ashbury district, the Summer of Love of 1967, Jimi Hendrix and Purple Haze, Jefferson Airplane and White Rabbit, the art of Peter Max, concert posters by Alton Kelley and Stanley "Mouse" Miller, and Timothy Leary promoting LSD as the way to drop out and turn on. They all converged into the psychedelic times of late sixties.

The baby boom had evolved into the Woodstock generation, and Chrysler marketing had a bold, unique way to capture sales from this group—the Mod Top option. Beginning in 1969, A-body Dodge Darts and Plymouth Barracuda coupes could get a vinyl top printed in a bright yellow Flower Power pattern. A second option could get that same material inset in the seats and door panels. Similar options were available for '69 Plymouth Satellites and '70 Barracudas, this time called Pop Prints, in a blue pattern. Dodge also had a green/gold Mod Top for '69 Darts and Coronets, and '70 Darts and Challengers. The patterns looked like they came from one of those miniskirts Judy Carne or Goldie Hawn wore on the groundbreaking *Rowan & Martin's Laugh-In* TV show. Actually it was something more familiar. Designer Jeffrey Godshall revealed the supplier of the vinyl material, Tuscany Plastics of New York City, also made vinyl tablecloths and shower curtains.

It was a brilliant move. Jack Smith, Plymouth's head of marketing, told a group of enthusiasts in 2000: "Mod Top was something that came out of my office. At the time psychedelic clothing and the whole spirit of Carnaby Street prevailed in the youth market. We tried to steal into that general emotional atmosphere, creating a paisley pattern that we used as a vinyl roof on a car with paint colors that complemented it."

Exterior Design had already done their job. With a $17.5 million budget, Plymouth Design began working on the second-generation Barracuda about the time the original car hit the showrooms in 1964, and while still based on the compact A-body platform, they sought to distance the new "fish" from its econo car roots. John Samsen, who played a major role in the first Barracuda, designed the second-gen car from the cowl forward, based on a concept by a young designer, John Herlitz. Milt Antonick did much of the rest of the fastback body, including the race-inspired exposed gas cap. Like the '67 Mustang it would compete against, the Barracuda would have coupe and convertible variants, as well as the original fastback body. Male buyers were targeted for the fastback, while females were the intent of the coupe, with the top and rear deck designed by Shunsuke "Matty" Matsuura. The new Barracuda was the first vehicle on Elwood Engle's watch to break outside the box, and the smooth, rounded shape drew positive press with references to European or Italian influences. *Car Life* magazine went so far as to proclaim the new Barracuda " . . . has a tautness of line and an integrity of design unmatched by few American cars of any vintage."

Under the hood, the base 273 V-8 in 1967 was replaced with a new 318 LA block engine the next year, along with a new performance LA 340, and the big-block 383 option. The performance 'Cuda model was added in '69, with 340, 383, and 440 powerplants. Despite the beautiful look and firepower under the hood, the 1967–1969 Barracuda never could capture the public's attention. Product planners had hoped to sell 100,000 Barracudas per year, but with new competition from Mercury's Cougar, GM's Camaro and Firebird, and even AMC's Javelin, Plymouth sold just over 126,000 in three

years. Of those, just 937 of the 31,977 Barracudas built in 1969 were Mod Tops, but it showed Chrysler was "with it" and they may well have sold more Plymouths because of it.

The Barracuda Mod Top in The Brothers Collection is hardly a muscle machine, and it wasn't intended to be. The Plymouth ad for the Pop Prints Satellite made it clear: "Your nearby Plymouth dealer will show you all our women-winning ways." The torque-heavy 318 two-barrel with automatic gives spirited performance, and the code Y2 Sunfire Yellow Barracuda with Mod Top option delivers a look that perfectly complements a tie-dyed shirt, fringed buckskin vest, bell-bottom jeans, and a set of love beads.

It's said that art imitates life, and the Mod Tops were uniquely a sign of their times.

"It has a tautness of line and an integrity of design

unmatched by few American cars of any vintage."

—*Car and Driver*

CHAPTER ELEVEN

1969 DODGE CHARGER DAYTONA 440

PRODUCTION

503

OPTIONS

C16 Console ($54.45)

C31 Left & Right Head
Restraints ($26.50)

S77 Power Steering ($100.00)

W21 Chrome Styled Steel
Wheels ($86.15)

Y2 Yellow Paint

C6X Black Vinyl Bucket
Seat Interior

HORSEPOWER

375 at 4,600 rpm

TORQUE

480 at 3,200 rpm

Deep within Chrysler's 3,850-acre Chelsea Proving Grounds is the 4.71-mile oval test track. The track is six lanes wide, each lane pitched at a greater angle than the previous one. The top lane is banked 36 degrees—higher than the Daytona International Speedway—and you need to be moving at over 100 miles per hour to stay in that slot. But on this day in 1969, the engineers on hand were seeing numbers so far beyond the century mark that it was staggering. The blue bullet in the top lane was streaking to 245 miles per hour on the straightaways! It was on this day the legend of the Dodge Charger Daytona was born.

The 1968 Ford Torinos and Mercury Cyclones easily handled Chrysler's '68 Chargers and Road Runners on the track. It had gotten so bad that Richard Petty defected to Ford for 1969. Then to assist Mr. Petty and the other FoMoCo drivers, Ford released the limited-production droop-nosed Torino Talladega and Cyclone Spoiler II models for the '69 season.

Bert Bouwkamp, Dodge's director of product planning in the sixties, told allpar.com: "Bob Rodger, our racing director (who worked for me at that time) came back from the Daytona 500 and said, 'NASCAR has gone "funny car" racing.' He said that we should design and build the ultimate race car and forget how practical it was or how it looked because we only had to build 500 of them to be approved by NASCAR as 'stock.' I got corporate approval to do that and we developed and built 500 Charger Daytonas in 1969."

Chrysler engineers estimated it would take 85 more horsepower to defeat the "funny" Ford competition, and the 426 Hemi was at about its limit within the rules. The only alternative was aerodynamics. A small team within Chrysler Engineering,

Continued on page 101

"Dodge's Daytona Charger wasn't designed for the street, but it has got to be the ultimate boulevard mind boggler of all time!"

—Hi-Performance CARS

Continued from page 97

Fluid Dynamics Laboratory manager Morgan Dawley and aerodynamicists Bob Marcel and Gary Romberg, had just a few weeks to develop a solution. Before the beginning of the 1969 NASCAR season, this team built a 3/8 model of a Dodge Charger, rented the wind tunnel at Wichita State University in Kansas, and developed the add-ons that became the Charger 500. The flush grille and flush rear window made the Charger competitive with the Talladega and Spoiler II, and Creative Industries built 500 of the requisite street Charger 500s to comply with NASCAR regulations.

It almost worked: "Charging" Charlie Glotzbach was leading the '69 Daytona 500 in Ray Fox's Charger 500, only to be slingshotted on the last lap by LeeRoy Yarbrough in his Ford. Then Ford released the Boss 429 "Semi-Hemi" engine in midseason, and the Charger 500 was hopelessly uncompetitive on the big tracks again.

Back to the wind tunnel for Dawley, Marcel, and Romberg. Using the same 3/8-scale model used for the Charger 500, they created the now-famous Daytona nose. The 0.28 coefficient of drag penetrated the air like a rocket and created so much downforce in front something needed to be done to the rear. The team tried a number of wings, settling for one 23 inches off the deck lid. This height kept the airfoil in the "clean" air above the roof, and still allowed the trunk lid to open. Front fender vents added tire clearance and extracted under-hood air. The Daytonas debuted at the inaugural Talladega 500 in September, and Charlie Glotzbach was told not to run faster than 185 miles per hour in practice to hide the superiority of the winged wonder. Instead he qualified at 199. The next day Daytonas swept the first four places. "From September 14 through the next year," Bert Bouwkamp recalled, Dodges and Plymouths "won forty-five out of the next fifty-nine races. I remember being at Charlotte Motor Speedway in the fall of 1969 watching our cars running first, second, third, and fourth in a diamond formation. They looked like the Blue Angels circling the speedway. I looked at Bob Rodger—our head of racing—and, although he was dying of leukemia, tears of joy were streaming down his cheeks."

All 1969 Dodge Charger Daytonas were built at Lynch Road Assembly, then sent to Creative Industries nearby for the installation of the Daytona nose, rear window, wing, and other aero pieces. A total of 503 Daytonas were built, and most, like this beautiful Y2 Yellow example in The Brothers Collection, were powered by the 375-horsepower 440 four-barrel (just 70 were Hemi equipped). They were expensive ($3,993) and weren't the most practical cars to drive on the street, but the attention the Daytona drew was (and is) nonstop.

Milt Antonick is quick to remind us that Design had nothing to do with creating the Daytona: it was strictly an Engineering project. True, but there is a certain beauty in an automobile built for speed and nothing else.

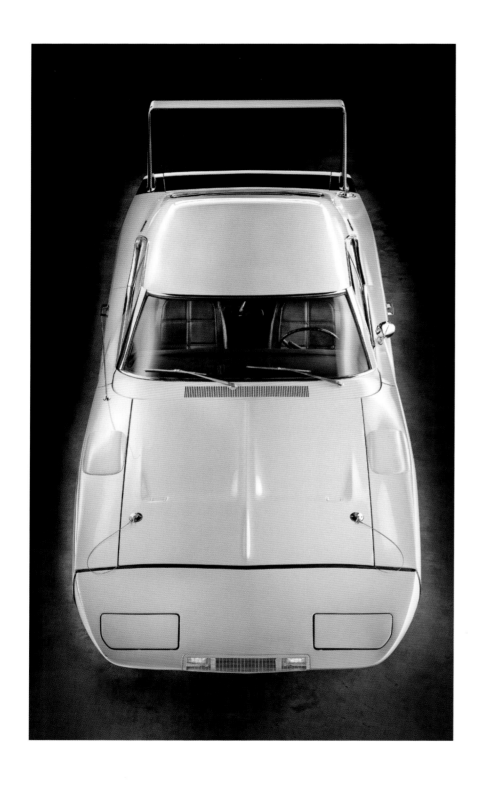

CHAPTER TWELVE

1970 PLYMOUTH HEMI 'CUDA COUPE

PRODUCTION 366

OPTIONS

E74 426 Hemi ($871.45)

D32 TorqueFlite 3-Speed Automatic Transmission ($227.05)

A01 Light Package ($36.00)

A36 3.55:1 Performance Axle Package ($64.40)

A62 Rallye Gauges ($76.75)

B51 Power Brakes ($42.95)

C16 Console ($53.35)

C62 6-Way Manual Seat ($32.20)

H31 Rear Window Defogger ($26.25)

J45 Hood Pins ($15.20)

P31 Power Windows ($105.20)

R35 Multiplex AM/FM Stereo Radio ($196.60)

P31 Power Windows ($105.20)

TX9 Black Velvet Paint

H6HW White Vinyl Interior

HORSEPOWER

425 at 5,000 rpm

TORQUE

490 at 4,000 rpm

When the 1964½ Mustang was introduced on April 17, 1964, Ford thought they had a nice economy commuter car on their hands. Buyers wanted more, and Ford had to eventually make the Mustang bigger in 1967 to give it the performance the public demanded. The new 1967 Camaro and Firebird were also designed around GM's big displacement engines. So the decisions made inside Highland Park in 1967 made total sense.

"As Director of Product Planning, I was the champion for the new 1970 'E' Body Barracuda/Challenger models," wrote Burt Bouwkamp in allpar.com. "At the Corporate Product Planning Committee Meeting, I promised management that we would

sell 200,000 cars a year. Manufacturing loved the plan because 200,000 cars a year was perfect—two 8-hour shifts at 60 cars/hour. Finance calculated that we would make money at 200,000 per year, and consequently the program was approved."

Rather than start with a compact platform the way Ford, GM, and even the first two Plymouth Barracudas did, the plan was to start with the Hemi-friendly confines of the B-body cars and heavily modify that into Chrysler's next pony car. "The 'B' engine option forced a wider car," Bouwkamp said. "Also we had to add width for provision for bigger wheels/tires. The additional width helped appearance, but of course it added weight and cost." But it allowed something under the long, wide hood the others could only dream of: the 426 Hemi engine.

The basic structure, including roof and doors, was developed at Advanced Design led by Cliff Voss. This was then released to the Plymouth and Dodge Studios for their individual skins. Over at the Plymouth Studio, it didn't go well at first. Designer John Samsen recalled to allpar.com: "El [Elwood Engel] came in on a late Friday afternoon. He didn't like the fender line on the clay model. 'Has anybody got a hammer?' he hollered. A modeler brought him one, and he proceeded to hammer down the top of the front fender. The union steward ran up to him and told him only union modelers were allowed to work on full-size clay. 'I'm not modeling; I'm hammering,' Elwood replied, and continued to pound the clay. 'Besides, I'm creating more work for you guys!' The steward backed off."

On another Saturday, still not pleased with the progress, Engel pointed to designer Milt Antonick and three clay modelers, "We're coming in tomorrow [Sunday] to design a car," Diren Yazejian told allpar.com about Engel's direction to the group. "On Monday morning, the body side of the '70 Barracuda, as we know it today, was ready for theme approval." Finally Elwood Engel was more than pleased. John Herlitz remembered, "Elwood was the first one to drive one of the early prototype cars off the elevator on the third floor of Building 128. And it was a Hemi. A green Hemi 'Cuda. And he got it angled around into the hallway that led down to the design auditorium, and he nailed that car on this parquet floor and just left these two black tracks down the hallway." The 'Cuda joined the Road Runner/GTX/Superbird and the new, compact Duster in Plymouth's Rapid Transit System, their most potent lineup ever.

"The restyled car is mean and lean this year, with bulges where they ought to be; the svelte fastback style has had its day," wrote *Motorcade*

Hemi-'Cuda 2-Door Hardtop.

'Cuda power.

This is 'Cuda. Our Rapid Transit System Barracuda.

'Cuda—one of three brand-new Barracuda models for 1970.

'Cuda gives you basically the same type of heavy-duty suspension system (torsion bars, shock absorbers, rear springs, anti-sway bars, frame, axle, etc.) as our bigger, intermediate-size cars.

'Cuda 340s and 383s even come equipped with a front and a rear anti-sway bar.

And in the case of our optional super-displacement 440 6-barrel engine, there's a "Shaker" hood scoop available—standard with Hemi engine.

And if you order the Hurst 4-speed floor-mounted shifter, you'll get a convenient "Pistol Grip" handle that makes shifting sharp and smooth.

Now, here are a few options that are particularly appropriate for 'Cuda.

Our Rallye instrument cluster which includes a 150 mph speedometer, oil pressure gauge, clock, trip odometer, and enormous tachometer.

Think about how you want us to build your 'Cuda and we'll build it that way. 'Cause 'Cuda makes it. Any way you like.

"Pistol-Grip" shift handle

magazine. "It's all business machine, with the long hood/short deck style reflected in its notchback design, a steeply raked windshield, and body-colored high density urethane foam Elastromeric [sic] front bumper." But the real fun was under the hood: "King Kong in a Barracuda isn't a monkey on your back—it's a hairy machine that commands respect, admiration, and awe. It's about as far as Plymouth people can go with their thunderous street Hemi engine, putting it in the revamped Barracuda ponycar, and they've turned it loose in the animal preserve this year." *Motor Trend* put one through its paces: "With the new Hemi 'Cuda, a quarter-mile goes by so fast you hardly knew it started. Even though our car had the widest optional F60 x 15 tire, we still experienced

considerable wheelspin, which cut E.T.S." They were still able to lay down a 13.7 at 101.2 miles-per-hour blast.

The code TX9 Black Velvet 'Cuda in The Brothers Collection is one of those cars that was ordered *just right*. It packs Hemi power, TorqueFlite trans, Drag-Pack 3:55:1 gears, and Shaker Hood, and just the goodies—Rallye gauges, six-way driver's seat, and power steering and brakes—to make it comfortable. It also has the rare rear window defogger, which makes it easier to watch the competition disappear.

Like brass knuckles hidden in a black velvet glove, this Hemi 'Cuda is sensuous, elegant, yet packs a knockout punch.

"King Kong in a Barracuda isn't a monkey on your back—it's a hairy machine that commands respect, admiration, and awe. It's about as far as Plymouth people can go with their thunderous street hemi engine . . . "

—*Motorcade*

CHAPTER THIRTEEN

1970 PLYMOUTH AAR 'CUDA

PRODUCTION

2,727

OPTIONS

D34 TorqueFlite Automatic ($216.20)

A01 Light Package ($36.00)

A62 Rallye Gauges ($90.30)

C62 6-Way Manual Seat ($33.30)

G34 Painted Remote Control Left Mirror ($15.15)

FJ4 Sassy Grass Green Paint

H6X9 Black Vinyl Interior

V6H Black Stripes

HORSEPOWER

290 at 5,000 rpm

TORQUE

345 at 3,400 rpm

"The potential of the Trans-Am series was fabulous, in my opinion," said Dan Gurney, one of America's greatest racers ever. "It was the very best kind of road racing that I can remember. All of the factories were behind us and we had the best drivers in this country competing. We also raced on all the best natural road circuits in North America, and unlike today, we had great fans who could really identify with the cars that were on the track."

It's said that racing improves the breed, but how often is that the case? When was the last time some piece of Formula 1, Top Fuel, or NASCAR technology found its way onto a street vehicle? That was the beauty of the Sports Car Club of America's Trans-Am series. The racers were mostly stock, and the rules were written to ensure the manufacturers made the same improvements to the showroom vehicles as on the racers. The series' 305-cubic-inch limit forced Chevrolet to create the Z/28 Camaro and Ford the Boss 302 Mustang, and the need for excellent cornering, braking, and aerodynamics gave these cars four-wheel disc brakes, heavy-duty suspensions, and the spoilers and aero tweaks that pushed the technology envelope of the late sixties. This gave

us arguably the best overall vehicles that Detroit produced during that time.

Even though a Dodge Dart won the Trans-Am championship in the series' inaugural year, 1966, a factory-backed effort didn't happen until 1970. At least when Chrysler jumped into the fray, they did it with both feet. Dan Gurney was lured away from Ford with tons of money, and his All American Racers team developed the Trans-Am cars and helped develop the accompanying street machines. Trans-Am rules dictated a production run of at least 2,500 units, or 0.4 percent of the brand's 1969 production, whichever was greater. The result for Chrysler-Plymouth showrooms: the 1970 AAR 'Cuda.

The AAR 'Cuda is one of those cars that just smacks you alongside the head. It's got a forward-tilting rake, caused by rear tires that are larger than the front. Those side pipes poking out from in front of those rear tires are real, as is the fiberglass hood with integral NACA duct and NASCAR-style hood pins. Under that hood was the real deal too, an updated version of the already excellent 340 V-8. In 1970, for the first time, the SCCA did not demand the street machines have the same 305 engine of the racers, so Chrysler could concentrate on using the 340 while developing a 305 for the race cars. The street AAR 'Cudas got a scaled-down 3x2 six-barrel system derived from the '69 A12 option, with a big air cleaner that sealed against the hood scoop. New cylinder heads with wider spacing for the pushrods were also added, along with a stronger block. The results: a 290-horsepower screamer.

Outside the AAR 'Cuda got a functional rear spoiler, front chin spoilers, remote control racing mirror, silver rocker panel caps, and bold graphics that matched Gurney's cars. This is style with substance, since under the sleek body is heavy-duty springs, power front disc brakes, the fine A833 four-speed transmission (A727 TorqueFlite automatic was optional), and an 8.75-inch Sure-Grip axle.

In testing, *Car and Driver* magazine's four-speed car saw 0–60 in 5.8 seconds, and 14.3 at 99.5 in the quarter. In 80-mile-per-hour braking stops, the AAR 'Cuda was superior to the Z28, Firebird Trans Am, and Boss 302.

1970 Plymouth Barracuda
Only the name is the same.

Plymouth makes it ♥

For all the promise of the AAR 'Cuda, the reality on the track was something else. Dan Gurney and teammate Swede Savage finished fifth in the championship in 1970, with no victories. Savage's best finish, a second, came at Road America in July, a track favoring high horsepower. Certainly the competition had a number of years of development over the AAR team, and you'd think by the next year Gurney and company would have been right in the mix, but Chrysler cancelled all factory racing programs except Richard Petty's after the '70 season.

The AAR 'Cuda in The Brothers Collection is a pristine example equipped with the optional automatic transmission. Gurney's racers were usually painted a dark blue with white graphics, so the graphics on some color combinations of production cars just don't look quite right. This one, painted in FJ4 Sassy Grass Green, nails it.

That solo year in Trans-Am gave us a 'Cuda with more than just straight-line bite. This time racing really did improve the breed.

"What will be built into all AAR 'Cudas, we must assume, is a kind of rough, hot rod flavor. . . . And if you look at the AAR 'Cuda as a ready-made street rod, what you see begins to make sense."

—*Car and Driver*

CHAPTER FOURTEEN

1970 PLYMOUTH SUPERBIRD

PRODUCTION

1

OPTIONS

358 cubic-inch Evernham
Dodge R5 Race Engine

Borg-Warner T-101 4-speed
Transmission

Magnum Force Tubular
K-frame with Tubular
Control Arms

Custom 4-link Rear Suspension
with 8¾-inch Rear End
with 3.90:1 Gears

15"x10" NASCAR
Race Wheels

BFGoodrich g-Force Race
and Street Tires

HORSEPOWER

780 at 8,500 rpm

TORQUE

n/a

Richard Petty had a problem. That meant Plymouth had a problem. Throughout the 1968 NASCAR season, Petty's Road Runner was uncompetitive on the larger speedways, thanks to the superior aerodynamics of Ford's Torinos. It was so bad that the '67 champion did not win a major event until October 27. Petty was not happy, and the prognosis for 1969 didn't look any better.

"Ford was always coming after me," Richard Petty told the British magazine *MotorSport* in 2014, "but we were really deep into our Chrysler deal. Then we found out that Chrysler was doing a wing car badged as a Dodge. So we went up to Detroit and said, 'What's Plymouth doing like this?' They said, 'Nothing. That's a Dodge, you're our Plymouth man.' I said, 'If you don't give me a wing car, I might go across the street.' They didn't seem to believe us, so we knocked on Ford's door, and at once we had a deal with Ford for '69."

Petty won the first race of the 1969 season, the Riverside 500. But Petty's team never fully came to grips with the Torino's handling, and Petty had a good, but not great, season. "Anyway, Chrysler realized they wanted us that much worse now, and the head of Plymouth came right down here to Level Cross himself.

Didn't bring no lawyers, didn't bring nobody. Just said, 'What will it take to get you back in a Plymouth? I said, 'Give me a wing.' So they did the Plymouth Superbird."

Lessons learned on the Charger Daytona could be applied to the Superbird, but since the Charger and the Road Runner did not share any sheet metal, an entirely new nose had to be developed. Plymouth engineers ended up using the hood and front fenders from the '70 Dodge Coronet, since the nose matched up better with their shape. Due to the different shape of the roof, the Superbird's rear wing sits farther back on the fenders and the side stabilizers are wider. Like the Daytona, the Plymouth's rear window was reshaped for better airflow. The nose was mocked up in clay, and low-volume kirksite dies were cast to form the steel nose. Creative Industries again built these limited-production automobiles.

Richard Petty did not win the Superbird's first superspeedway race, the 1970 Daytona 500. Petty dropped out on the seventh lap, but his teammate, young New Englander Pete Hamilton, took home the trophy over David Pearson in a Mercury. Petty may well have won yet another championship had it not been for a serious crash at Darlington, which kept

him on the sidelines for a number of months. Then for 1971 NASCAR banned all "funny cars" from all manufacturers. That's okay—Petty won his third championship that year anyway.

Thanks to a NASCAR rule change for 1970, 1,935 Superbirds were built. Most were equipped with the standard 440 four-barrel, but 716 were ordered with the 440 Six-Barrel, and 315 were Hemi powered. Options were limited, and air conditioning and the Air Grabber hood were not available. Base price was expensive, $4,298, and the Hemi added $841.05. The only colors available were EW1 Alpine White, EK2 Vitamin C Orange, FY1 Lemon Twist, FJ5 Lime Light, EB5 Blue Fire Metallic, EV2 Tor Red, and B3 Corporate Blue (as close to the famed Petty Blue as you can get).

The Superbird in The Brothers Collection is not an original NASCAR 'Bird, but a modern tribute to those dominating racers. Built in 2008 by YearOne's Ghostworks Garage, the Superbird was created by football player/wrestler/TV personality Bill Goldberg to benefit the work of former drag racing champion Darryl Gwynn. Starting with a '70 Belvedere, the car was modified to 1970 NASCAR specs patterned after the actual race cars in the Talladega Motor Speedway Museum. "Goldberg said he wanted it to be as close to a

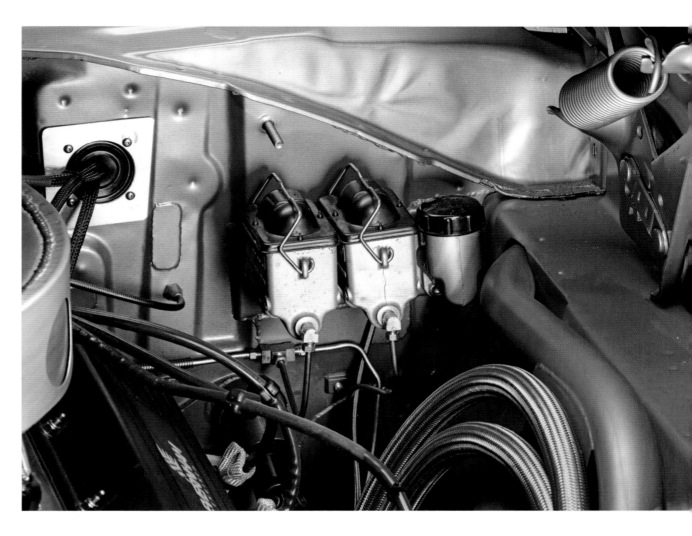

real NASCAR racer as possible, for the street," said YearOne project designer Phil Brewer. That included a simplified seventies-era roll cage, and, of course, reproduction Superbird body panels.

Instead of a 426 Hemi under the hood, Gillette-Evernham Racing donated one of their R5 358 cubic-inch engines that was in use by the Dodge NASCAR teams in 2008. Though detuned for pump fuel, the engine still made 780-horsepower on the dyno. Modern coil-over suspension and four-wheel disc brakes rounded out the package.

RTM Productions documented the Superbird's construction on their *MuscleCar TV* and *PowerBlock* shows, and it was displayed at the SEMA show in the fall of 2008. Then on January 18, 2009, Barrett-Jackson auctioned the Ghostworks Superbird for $551,100, with all proceeds going to the Darryl Gwynn Foundation's efforts on severe spinal cord injury research.

Almost forty years later, the Plymouth Superbird is still a winner.

" 'What will it take
to get you back in
a Plymouth?' I said,
'Give me a wing'.
So they did the
Plymouth Superbird."

– *Richard Petty in* MotorSport

CHAPTER FIFTEEN

PRODUCTION 19

OPTIONS

E74 426 Hemi ($841.05)

D34 TorqueFlite 3-Speed
Automatic (N/C)

A36 Performance Axle
Package ($64.40)

C16 Console ($54.45)

G31 Manual Outside Right
Mirror ($6.85)

J25 3-Speed Wipers (N/C)

N85 Tachometer (N/C)

R11 Music Master AM Radio
($61.55)

EB3 Light Blue Metallic Paint

C6XA Black Vinyl Bucket
Seat Interior

V8W White R/T Stripe

HORSEPOWER

425 at 5,000 rpm

TORQUE

490 at 4,000 rpm

1970 DODGE CHARGER R/T HEMI

There is one thing about success—you don't mess with it. Dodge didn't.

The 1968 Dodge Charger had a 586 percent increase in sales over the '67 fastback. So for 1969, Dodge wisely left it mostly untouched. What little they messed with arguably made the car even better. Diran Yazejian designed a new split grille for the '69 Charger and designed full-width taillights that flowed beautifully with Richard Sias's sheet metal. As iconic as the '68 Charger was, the '69 was equally iconic in its own way. Sales were slightly less than the previous year—85,680 vs. 92,590—but a great success nonetheless.

One new version of the '69 Charger was the Charger 500 built specifically to address the aerodynamic deficiencies of the '68 car. The one and only reason for the Charger 500 was NASCAR, but that made for an interesting street machine, as

Car Life found out. "The Crown Comes Back" read the headline. "A four-speed Dodge Hemi Charger 500 takes the title of quickest test car. The automatic version wasn't far behind." That caught everyone's attention. They continued: "Dodge sent a team—two Charger 500s, both Hemi-powered. One had a stick shift and the other an automatic. The four-speed car, showroom stock right down to its tires and 3.55:1 axle ratio, turned an E.T. of 13.68. The automatic—and mind, this is a car Mom could drive to bingo games—clocked a 13.92 sec. E.T." Just in case the road to bingo isn't straight, "the Chargers were more than just dragstrip terrors. On the handling course, they slammed through turns like the disguised NASCAR racers they really are, both drivers secure in the knowledge that they could run in close company because the cars would cover for human mistakes. In town, they responded to command, stuck to the road through rain and mud, and came through an hour-long freeway snarl without so much as a fouled sparkplug."

Thankfully, for 1970, Dodge again left well enough alone. Diran Yazejian again did his update magic, giving the Charger a "loop" front bumper that was becoming the design language of the future for Chrysler products. The new front did little for the aerodynamics, but the 1969 Charger 500 and Daytona models were again dominating the racetracks of the nation in 1970, so it didn't matter. Yazejian also changed up the double-side C scallops into a large single indent. R/T models got a single reverse faux scoop that covered the front of the C surface treatment. The 440 six-pack engine was added, but otherwise that was pretty much the same Dodge Charger America came to know and love. Charger sales did drop off to 46,315 for 1970, but sales of all performance cars in 1970 was about half the previous year's.

The '69 Charger was the ride of choice of the Duke Boys in the 1979–1985 TV series *The Dukes of Hazzard*. It's too bad the popular TV show came out ten years after the Charger featured in it, or sales might have exploded the way *Smokey and the Bandit* sparked a demand for Pontiac Firebirds. But when Chrysler's Head of Design Ralph Gilles—today's Elwood Engle—and his team wanted to update the current Dodge Charger, what was their inspiration? Look at a 2012 or newer Charger: the large C-shaped indent

Continued on page 134

"The Chargers were more than just dragstrip terrors. On the handling they really are, both drivers secure in the knowledge that they could run

course, they slammed through turns like the disguised NASCAR racers in close company because the cars would cover for human mistakes."

—*Car Life*

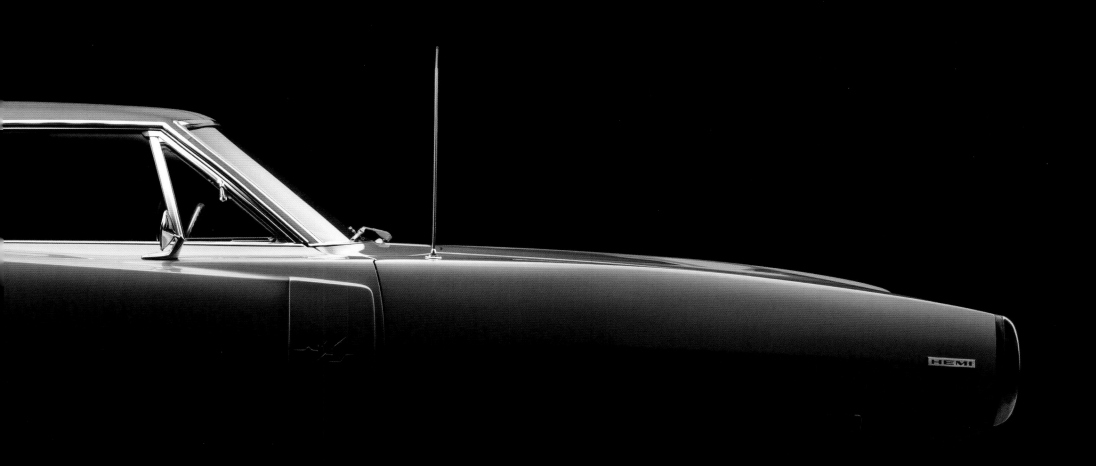

Continued from page 130

and full-width Raceway taillight spell one thing—1970 Charger. That is the strength of the Richard Sias original design, and Diran Yazejian's changes. Each year is slightly different, and everyone seems to prefer one over the other two, but each is distinctly Charger.

There are signs along the roads of the Lone Star state that read "Don't Mess With Texas." And in Tyler, Texas, there was a Dodge Charger that nobody messed with. It was ordered with all the right stuff: power steering and brakes, TorqueFlite automatic, and the Performance Axle Package with 3.55:1 gears. This was the same powertrain that *Car Life* crowned their "quickest test car." Fancy wheels just added weight, so 15X7 painted-steel

wheels with "dog dish" caps were fine. And for Texas-sized power, the 426 Hemi was specified. It was dressed in code EB3 Light Blue Metallic paint and the white R/T stripe.

That Hemi Charger now resides in The Brothers Collection. Only 112 Hemi Charger R/Ts were ordered in 1970, just 19 of those with TorqueFlite. Research shows this is probably the only one of those built with EB3 Light Blue Metallic paint. It has just over 77,500 miles and has never been restored.

"There's just something about it, you know it's a Charger," Richard Sias said recently. "It's got character. It's got that giddy-up-and-go." Like success and Texas, some things shouldn't be messed with.

PRODUCTION

2,399

OPTIONS

A53 Challenger T/A Package
($865.70)

D34 TorqueFlite Automatic
Transmission ($216.20)

C16 Console ($53.35)

B51 Power Brakes ($42.95)

J78 Front Spoiler ($20.95)

S77 Power Steering ($90.35)

FM3 Panther Pink

H6X6 Black Vinyl Interior

V6H Black Stripes

HORSEPOWER

290 at 5,000 rpm

TORQUE

345 at 3,400 rpm

CHAPTER SIXTEEN

1970 DODGE CHALLENGER T/A

Dodge and Chrysler-Plymouth dealers were always at odds. Whatever Plymouth had, Dodge dealers wanted, even though they had their unique Charger. In 1970, Dodge finally got their very own pony car, the Challenger.

Though very similar to the '70 Barracuda, the Challenger was envisioned to be upscale, the same way the Mercury Cougar was an upscale Mustang. Chrysler engineers gave the Challenger a 110-inch wheelbase, which gave the rear seat passenger 2 more inches of room over the Plymouth. Challenger also had a unique body. Burt Bouwkamp told allpar.com, "The Challenger plan was always to share door openings, windshield, cowl, and platform with Barracuda. We also intended to share door outer skins, but during clay model development we decided that this interchangeability formula limited achieving a unique appearance for Challenger so the door skins became unique. The rest of the interchangeability with Barracuda was in line with the original product plan. Challenger by plan had 2 to 3

inches more wheelbase (ala Dart vs. Valiant) than Barracuda and was also planned to have a $100 higher market price."

Carl Cameron told *Muscle Car Review* magazine about the Challenger design: "It was [Bill] Brownlie's body side, which is the section through the door, that was selected. To understand how significant the difference was between the Barracuda and the Challenger, consider the car as a loaf of bread, and remove a slice from the center. This slice is called a body section. The Barracuda's body section was clean and simple in the sense that it came right off the beltline, went out to a peak, and went right underneath with extreme tumble under. The Challenger's body section shows it kicked out a little more than the Barracuda, came down at an angle, flared out to the character line, and then back down and into the sill."

Carl Cameron contributed the Challenger's front end, which used four headlights to the Barracuda's two to imply the upscale nature of the Dodge. "I did the grille very deep," Cameron said.

"The Challenger was very flat-faced. There was not a very large physical air opening in that car. The lights were set back at an angle to funnel the air into that center opening." The rear end also had a unique Cameron touch, the backup lights. "It had the name 'Dodge' in it. That was the first time anyone had put a name in a backup lamp." The upscale image the designers wanted must have worked—Challengers outsold Barracudas 83,012 to 50,617 in 1970.

Dodge also got to go Trans-Am racing in the epic 1970 season. They contracted with Autodynamics in Marblehead, Massachusetts, to run the Trans-Am program. Autodynamics, founded by Ray Caldwell in 1962, was the world's largest race car manufacturer at the time, selling hundreds of Formula Vee racers for SCCA amateur racing. They had also built a fairly successful Cam Am racer in 1969. With Sam Posey at the helm, and a Challenger built by Dan Gurney's All American Racers, the team was posed for success. The Challenger, painted the High Impact Paint color Sublime, was driven by Sam Posey to three third-place finishes in 1970—at Road America; Kent, Washington; and Posey's "home" track, Lime Rock—and third place in the championship. Sadly, 1970 was the only year of the Challenger Trans-Am program.

To meet the SCCA's production requirements, the Challenger T/A (for Trans-Am) was created. Dodge's press release revealed, "The engine will be a special 340-cubic-inch powerplant with three two-barrel carburetion, modified block, special

cylinder heads and a modified valve train. The block has been reinforced in the main bearing webs, and the special cylinder head casting has been modified to provide better intake ports and accommodate a longer pushrod. The valve train has been modified to accept a slightly different angle on the pushrod, and a special camshaft. The car will have a special side exhaust, low-restriction dual exhaust system with two single-pass mufflers located ahead of the axle. The exhaust outlets will emerge under the side sills ahead of the

rear wheel openings." The Challenger T/A was identical to the AAR 'Cuda in most respects, including the powerful 290-horsepower 340 six-barrel engine; only the hood scoop was different.

The Challenger T/A in The Brothers Collection is painted a High Impact Paint color that debuted in the spring of 1970, code FM3 Panther Pink. Not every man can own a pink muscle car, but 290 horsepower, a four-speed trans, 3.91 gears, and a race-bred chassis are huge confidence builders, aren't they?

"We found the new Challenger extremely comfortable to drive, and to handle exceptionally well by all but the most nitpicking yeah-but-have-you-ever-driven-a-Porsche standards."

– Road Test

CHAPTER SEVENTEEN

1970 DODGE SUPER BEE 440 SIX-PACK

PRODUCTION

97

OPTIONS

E87 440 Six-Pack Engine
($249.55)

D21 4-Speed Manual
($197.25)

A34 Super Track Pack 4.10:1
Dana 60 ($235.65)

B41 Front Disc Brakes
($27.90)

B51 Power Brakes ($42.95)

G33 Remote Left Mirror ($10.45)

N96 Ramcharger Hood Scoop
($73.30)

S77 Power Steering ($105.20)

W21 14X7 Rally Wheels ($43.10)

FY1 Top Banana High-Impact
Paint ($14.05)

M6XW Black/White
Bucket Seats

V6W White Longitudinal
Tape Stripe

HORSEPOWER

390 at 4,700 rpm

TORQUE

490 at 3,600 rpm

Chrysler President Lynn Townsend's message to Burt Bouwkamp, then thirty-eight and a newly appointed manager at Chrysler was simple: Think Pontiac. "He wanted to be sure that I got the message that there was a new market plan for Dodge," Bouwkamp said. "For the next year the Dodge dealers took every opportunity to tell the management they wanted to sell in the Ford-Chevrolet-Plymouth market."

So when Plymouth uncaged the Road Runner in 1968, and sales were beyond belief, Dodge dealers had to have one too. Creating it was easy, essentially a Road Runner with Coronet sheet metal. Giving it a personality was the challenge. Graphic designer Harvey Winn designed the logo, then carved the three-dimensional badge on his kitchen table—Super Bee. It was brilliant—a tough killer bee with goggles, zoomie headers, and a helmet—and it didn't cost a penny in licensing from a

Hollywood studio. The origin of the name? Well, it's a B-body car, isn't it?

Dodge released the Super Bee in the spring of 1968, and the dealers were happy: 7,842 sold that year, and with more options and their own version of the A12 440 six-pack in 1969, another 26,125. Of course, Dodge also had a runaway hit in the Charger, so combined, Dodge Fever and their Scat Pack performance cars had indeed gone viral.

"Dodge introduces a new model Super Bee at a new lower price. $3,074.00." That's what the Super Bee ad in the car magazines said in 1970. "That's $64 dollars less than last year's standard hot dog hardtop." No Dodge Fever girl. No mention of horsepower or performance. Just your basic Coronet with a 383 Magnum and three-speed for $3,074. What happened to the fever?

Change was in the air, no doubt about it. They could see the monthly sales numbers in Highland Park, and their best-selling performance cars from 1969 were selling at about half that volume in 1970. The same thing was happening over at GM and Ford. It was time to appeal on another level: price. Now, $64 in 1970 was a decent chunk of change—about $400 today—and Dodge achieved that price by substituting a three-speed manual for the usual four-speed.

The problem wasn't the '70 Super Bee, or even the price. It really was a special machine, with a fresh design by Diran Yazejian that separated it from the Road Runner in no uncertain terms. Loop bumpers were becoming a design theme across all Chrysler brands, and the '70 Coronet sported not one, but two loop bumpers. Yazejian's original theme, drawn in March 1967, called for twin swept-back body-colored nostrils. A drawing made in September was closer to the production version.

"When we were working out the design on the full-size clay model," Yazejian recalled, "I originally tapered the loops around an imaginary horizontal line bisecting the dual headlights, so each loop tapered in two directions—up and down. But this didn't look right, so instead, I kept the bottom line of the loops horizontal—like my original green-and-black sketch—and restricted the tapering to the upper half of the loops. This made the design 'read right.' " Out back Yazejian echoed the front with segmented delta-shaped taillights, an update of his '69 Coronet design. He proposed those taillights work sequentially, like the Cougar and Thunderbird's had, but that was shot down for cost reasons. It's been suggested Diran Yazejian was influenced by the shape of bee's wings in designing the '70 Coronet. Love it or hate it, it was a distinctive and memorable design.

Out in the asphalt jungle, the Super Bee made itself known in another way. "In its element, meaning on the strip, the 'Bee was so good that it

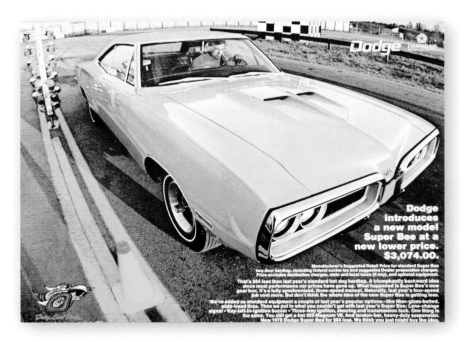

Dodge
introduces
a new model
Super Bee at a
new lower price.
$3,074.00.

was almost a drag (sorry)," wrote *Car Life*. "It ran with so little ceremony that it was like driving a family car." Zero to 60 in 6.3 seconds, the quarter in 13.8 at 104.2 (with two passengers and test equipment), and a top speed of over 117 miles per hour. That's some trip to Grandma's.

The '70 Super Bee in The Brothers Collection is one of those unmistakable killer street machines. Packing 440 six-pack sting through a four-speed and 4.10:1 gears, this 25,800-mile 'Bee is ready for flight. It looks the part in code FY1 Top Banana Yellow with white stripes and black and white vinyl interior.

This 1970 440 six-pack Super Bee is clearly the top banana of the asphalt jungle.

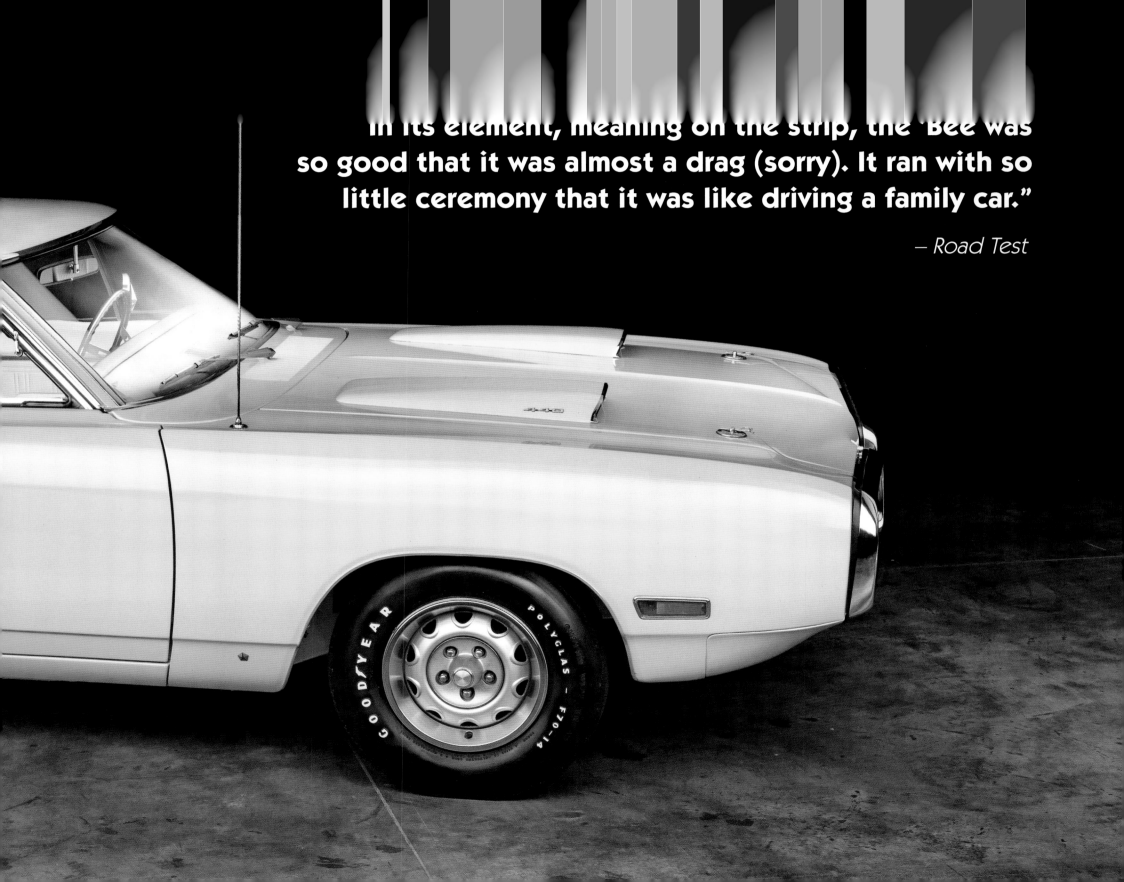

In its element, meaning on the strip, the 'Bee was so good that it was almost a drag (sorry). It ran with so little ceremony that it was like driving a family car."

— *Road Test*

OPTIONS

E55 340 4-BBL

D32 TorqueFlite 3-Speed
Automatic ($216.20)

A01 Light Package ($36.00)

A21 Elastomeric Front Bumper
($68.00)

A62 Rallye Instrument Cluster
($90.30)

B51 Power Brakes ($42.95)

C16 Console ($53.35)

C62 Comfort Position 6-Way
Seat Adjuster ($33.30)

G36 Color-Keyed Remote
Left and Manual Right Mirrors
($26.10)

H51 Air Conditioning ($357.65)

J45 Hood Pins ($15.40)

L34 Fog Lights ($21.05)

M26 Wheel Moldings ($7.60)

M31 Belt Moldings ($13.60)

M91 Luggage Rack ($31.30)

N95 California Evaporative
Emissions Controls ($37.85)

P31 Power Windows ($105.20)

P37 Power Convertible Top
($52.85)

EB5 Blue Fire Metallic Paint

H6B5 Blue Vinyl Bucket Seats

V3W White Convertible Top

HORSEPOWER

275 at 5,000 rpm

TORQUE

340 at 3,200 rpm

CHAPTER EIGHTEEN

1970 PLYMOUTH 'CUDA 340 CONVERTIBLE

Some sixties performance cars were designed for Lions Drag Strip, and that's fine. But by the end of the decade, some were more geared toward Sunset Boulevard. They still had some major pop under the hood, but they made the ride so much more enjoyable. The 1970 'Cuda 340 is a perfect example.

"Beware the Quiet Fish," said *Hot Rod* in its January '71 issue. "Plymouth's Barracuda is offered in many configurations, but there's one that is best of all: the 'Cuda 340. What this car does is deliver a no-compromise performance exhibition at all stages, be it handling, drag racing, street riding, or cross-country junketing." The 'Cuda 340 " . . . is a far better-driving machine than either the 440 or 426 V-8-equipped 'Cudas, and at least equals the performance you might expect from an assembly-line-stock Hemi 'Cuda. Both the larger engines cost several hundred dollars more, weight is greater, and the cost

of operating is a little harder to live with than with the 340." That was a bold claim, but accurate, as *Hot Rod*'s Steve Kelly and John Dianna discovered at Lions Drag Strip. Their best time, 14.18 sec. at 100.33 miles per hour, while not quite A12 Road Runner territory, was still darn quick, and it "does beat a stock Z28 or Boss 302 (at least the ones we've tested) through a quarter-mile," Steve Kelly and John Dianna wrote. Dianna must have been impressed, because he began drag racing a 340 Duster as a personal project with record-breaking consistency a year later.

The secret to the 340's performance? Development Engineer Charles "Pete" Hagenbuch told allpar.com: "As for design, all I can tell you is big valves, a big cam, and a high compression ratio. . . . The 340 was like the [Pontiac] 389; we threw the book at it and most of it worked. But it was still a wedge head, and it wasn't magical. But it sure did feel good." Hagenbuch was one of those unsung heroes who saw it all—from 1958 to 1987 he worked in valvetrain, performance, emissions, and other areas on Chrysler's most legendary engines including the 426 Hemi, the B/RB series big-blocks, the LA small blocks, and more.

The beautiful 'Cuda 340 convertible, painted EB5 Blue Fire Metallic (the legendary B5 Blue), in The Brothers Collection is perfect for Sunset Boulevard—or the back lots of Paramount Studio. Supercar dealer (and Motorbooks author) Colin Comer owned this 'Cuda 340 for about five years. "I don't know if it was given or loaned to them, but I have a copy of the original warranty book showing that Chrysler's West Coast promo office delivered the car to Aaron Spelling Productions, Inc., on October 22, 1969," he said.

The 'Cuda was thought to have been used on the popular ABC TV show *The Mod Squad*, a police drama about three hip criminals who escaped prosecution to go undercover in L.A. The show ran from 1968 to 1973, and in later years the characters in *The Mod Squad*—actors Michael Cole as Pete, Clarence Williams III as Linc, and Peggy Lipton as Julie—often drove a gold-and-black Challenger convertible. Why the show's producer had this 'Cuda seems a mystery. Comer explained, "I bought the car from its second owner, or so I recall, who told me the car couldn't have been used on the show since *The Mod Squad* used a Challenger—but I think they may have used it for through-the-windshield interior shots perhaps. There were holes in the cowl that I suspected were for camera mounts." Now it makes more sense. If all the

camera showed was the familiar E-body cowl and windshield along with the occupants, the color of the car and the fact it was a 'Cuda and not a Challenger wouldn't matter.

At least *The Mod Squad* fought crime in comfort. This ragtop is fully loaded, including six-way seat, console, light group, and power windows, brakes, and steering. The luggage rack might look like a questionable accessory, until you open the trunk—Plymouth even boasted the 'Cuda trunk was the smallest of all ponycars. It also has the cool body-color Elastomeric front bumper and air conditioning, which is perfect for those SoCal days when the hot Santa Ana winds push temperatures over 100 degrees.

For all the fast, fun versatility of the 1970 Plymouth E-body, you would think more than just 155 'Cuda 340 convertibles would have been built. But the total for all the 'Cuda variants—340, 383, 440, and Hemi—was just 550.

Speed, style, and comfort, the 1970 'Cuda 340 convertible was the perfect way to fight crime on TV—or the traffic on the Hollywood freeway.

Plymouth's Barracuda is offered in many configurations, but there's one that is best of all: the 'Cuda 340. What this car does is deliver a no-compromise performance exhibition at all stages, be it handling, drag racing, street riding, or cross-country junketing."

– Hot Rod

PART 3

RAPID

Chrysler Corporation had not only survived the sixties, but it looked to be in fine shape. The Plymouth Road Runner and second-generation Dodge Charger had been outstanding successes. The E-body Challenger and Barracuda had filled a market need and were seeing decent sales. In the overall US market share picture, Chrysler held pretty much steady at 14.9 percent. GM was down a resounding 10 percent in share, but that was deceiving since they had been crippled by a six-month labor stoppage. Ford was up over 4.4 percent, but some of that may have been due to GM's woes.

But one number sent shivers throughout Chrysler's Highland Park headquarters. Despite having the biggest and best lineup of performance cars in its history, sales for those cars in 1970 were half of 1969's figure.

Part of the cause was the rapid increase in insurance premiums in recent years since people and property were getting maimed or worse by cars with enormous engines. Our representatives in Washington created the National Highway Traffic Safety Administration and the Clean Air Act in 1970, and manufacturers were having to devote more resources and money to meeting upcoming pollution and fuel economy regulations. Just as important, the peak of the baby boom was now in their mid-twenties, settling down, and having families. The times were changing, but no one knew just how. Rather than wring their hands, Chrysler leadership charged into 1971 with what helped get them there—performance.

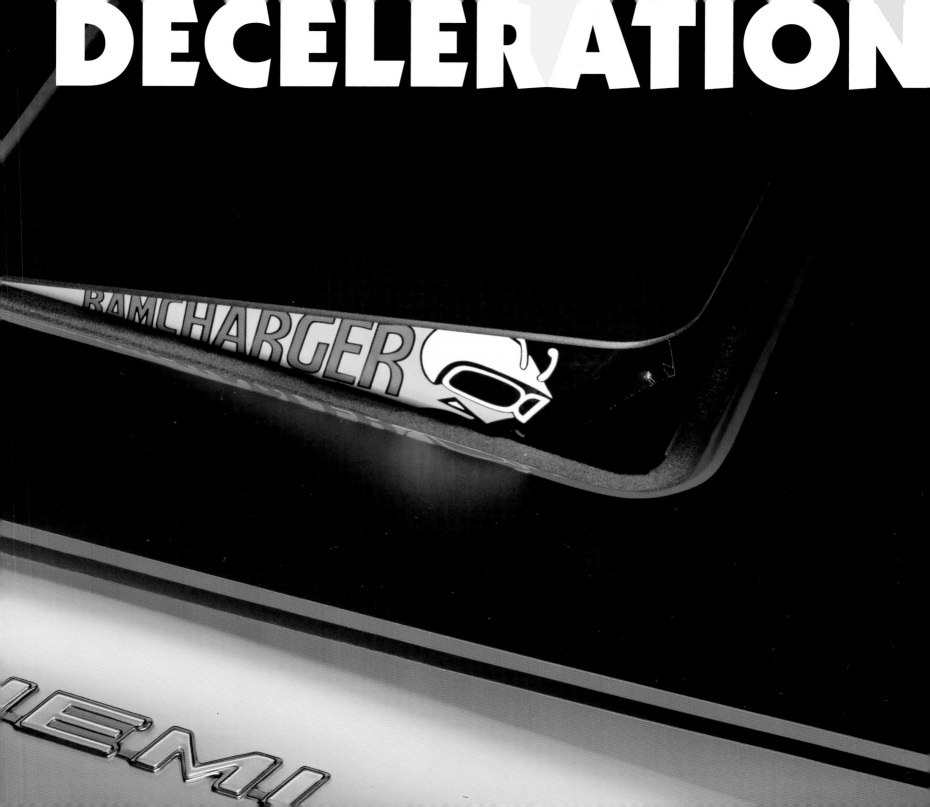

DECELERATION

CHAPTER NINETEEN

PRODUCTION
30

OPTIONS

E74 426 Hemi ($746.50)

D21 4-Speed Manual
Transmission (N/C)

FE5 Bright Red Paint

D5X9 Black Cloth
& Vinyl Interior

V1X Black Vinyl Top

HORSEPOWER

425 at 5,000 rpm

TORQUE

490 at 4,000 rpm

1971 DODGE CHARGER R/T 426 HEMI PILOT CAR

"A Dodge Charger? A piece of sculpture? . . . Brownlie and his associates have come up with the best-styled new car for 1971. The Charger comes off as anything but a styling compromise. Not only is it apparent to people viewing the car from the outside, but the driver is aware that he is controlling something far from normal as well." That's what *Car and Driver* said of the new 1971 Dodge Charger. After three years of styling leadership, the new Charger had a tough act to follow. Design Chief Bill Brownlie and his team gave the '71 a totally new design, with sleek fuselage styling that looked much different from the former models, yet keeping familiar Charger design clues. *Motor Trend* included the '71 Charger in its Car of the Year voting, saying "It was evident, after the initial success of the '68-'70 Chargers, the Dodge stylists would have to burn some midnight oil to create a fresh approach that would again make Charger something unique in an industry where very little is unique."

Long before the first '71 Chargers arrived at dealerships, even long before Job One came off the Lynch Road line, a Bright Red Charger R/T Hemi rode down that same assembly line. Known as Job Number Twenty-Nine, it was one of a group of pilot cars built in early 1970—the first '71 Hemi Charger.

Pilot cars are built on the assembly lines that will ultimately produce the vehicles, but many months before actual production starts. Production stops, and twenty or twenty-five of the next year's models are built by the same people who will eventually assemble them. It's an opportunity for Engineering to verify that years of development will all come together properly. It also gives the assembly personnel some experience building the new car, and possibly give feedback on improving the process. It's an annual ritual on most assembly lines.

Job Number Twenty-Nine was packed with many options. Most notable is the 426 Hemi with A833 4-speed producing

425 horsepower, the only engine in Chrysler's 1971 lineup to not experience a loss of horsepower. Outside, the Charger featured a black vinyl roof, black R/T graphics, hideaway headlights, color-keyed racing mirrors, bumper guards, and rare wide chrome door and window moldings. Inside was a black hound's-tooth cloth interior with deluxe light group, rear speaker, and rear defogger. No wheel covers were installed; maybe the final production pieces were not ready, but it could be they were not important to the pilot run and excluded.

But Job Number Twenty-Nine, being a preproduction car, has some unusual equipment. The instrument panel is a strange mix of standard and Strato-Vent dash with custom handmade vents and incomplete ductwork. The rear springs are '70 units, and the doors are prototype pieces with nonstandard hinges and are missing the "X" braces. The trunk lid is also missing the mounts for the optional rear spoiler. Handwritten notes to the assembly personnel were also found in the doors. Finally, it has those frustrating left/right-threaded wheel lugs that Chrysler products had on prior models, but eliminated for '71.

What happens to those pilot cars? Some get cut up by Engineering to ensure dimensions are correct and spot welds are sound. Others are beat unmercifully at the Proving Grounds to search for potential flaws. No matter what the use, the pilot cars and all other test vehicles are destroyed right at the Proving Grounds to prevent potentially damaged or compromised cars or components from getting into the public's hands.

So the mystery is, just how did Job Number Twenty-Nine get spared from the scrap bailer? Somehow it made it to Mr. Norm's Grand Spaulding Dodge in Chicago, where it was sold in 1973. Thankfully, everyone who owned Job Number Twenty-Nine recognized it as something special and preserved its unique features. Then a few years ago, master Mopar restorer Roger

Gibson had the honor of spending two years bringing it back to its as-built splendor. "It has the original engine and transmission, and is finished in the factory color," Gibson said. "Typical for a pilot car, it had a blank fender tag, so we had to pay close attention as we disassembled it. We were meticulous; we kept detailed records of all the special features in order to preserve everything as it was. For instance, we found 'job #29' hand-written on many components."

A total of thirty 1971 Dodge Charger R/Ts were produced with the 426 Hemi and four-speed. But the Bright Red Charger in The Brothers Collection isn't one of them. It's Job Number Twenty-Nine—the mysterious pilot car that escaped the crusher.

"A Dodge Charger? A piece of sculpture? The Charger comes to people viewing the car from the outside but the driver is

off as anything but a styling compromise. Not only is it apparent
aware that he is controlling something far from normal as well."

—*Car and Driver*

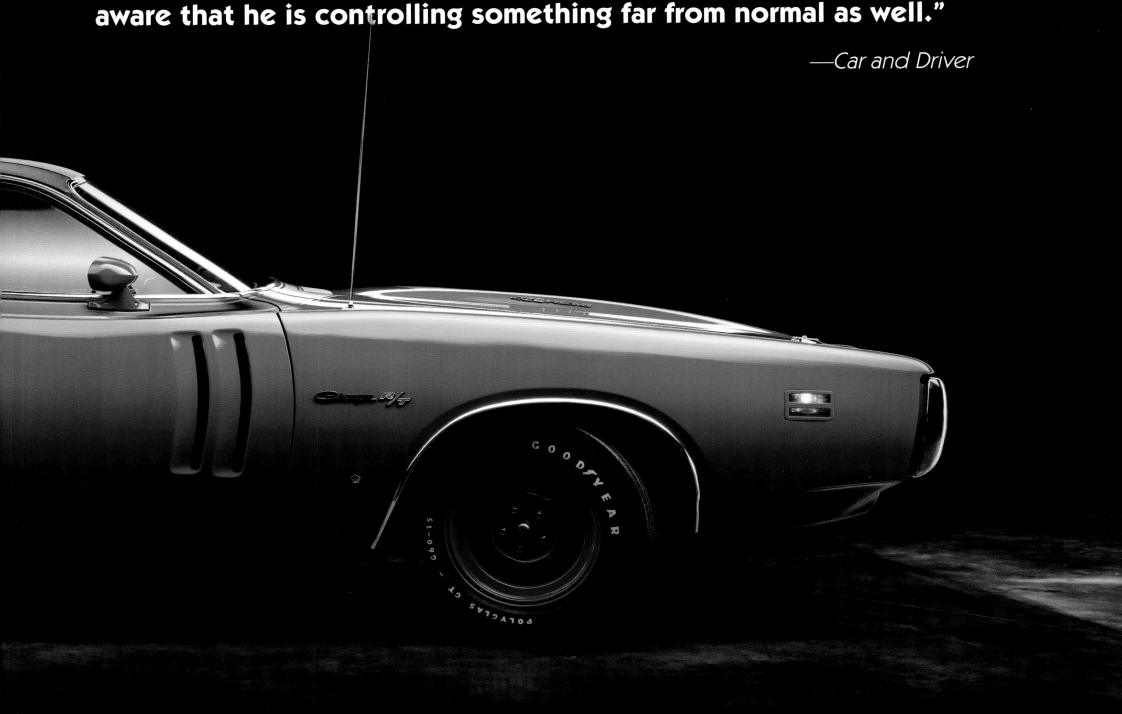

CHAPTER TWENTY

1971 DODGE CHALLENGER R/T 440+6

OPTIONS

E87 440+6 Engine ($253.20)

D32 TorqueFlite 3-Speed
Automatic ($229.35)

A34 Super Track Pak ($201.75)

B51 Power Brakes ($41.55)

C16 Console ($53.05)

G11 Tinted Glass ($36.85)

G31 Chrome Outside Right
Racing Mirror ($10.80)

G33 Chrome Outside Left
Racing Mirror ($14.95)

J25 Variable Speed Wipers
($10.60)

J45 Hood Pins ($15.20)

J46 Locking Fliptop Gas Cap
($7.75)

N96 Shaker Hood Fresh Air
Package ($94.00)

TX9 Black Paint

H6X9 Black Vinyl Interior

V-6V Orange Stripes

HORSEPOWER

390 at 5,200 rpm

TORQUE

490 at 3,200 rpm

"To understand the Challenger you first better know a little bit about Chrysler Corporation and its strategies," wrote *Car and Driver* in 1970. "Chrysler can't do anything first. Instead, it carefully watches what everybody else in Detroit is doing, and when it sees an area of abnormal market activity, it leaps exactly onto the spot. Because it always leaps late—which is inevitable if it doesn't begin to prepare its entry into the market until someone else already has one—it tries to make up for being late by jumping into said spot harder than everybody else. That is why you didn't see a real Chrysler sporty car until 1970 (and that is why Chrysler's small car will be lucky to see light of day in 1971)."

Apparently *Car and Driver* missed two unique Chrysler innovations that stormed the market, the 1968–1970 Dodge Charger and the 1968–1970 Plymouth Road Runner, both of which had no real competition from GM or Ford. Other publications were much more positive about the Challenger. Over at *Road Test* magazine, their time spent with a '70 Challenger powered by the 440 six-pack was apparently much different. They had some minor complaints too, like rear visibility, "but once by these points of argument we had a great deal of fun driving the new Dodge. Whether or not it is all worth the $5,210 price tag is a question between your conscience and your finance company." They found the 440 six-pack " . . . a whole lot of car to drive, sometimes in a frightening way. With normal throttle, it travels around city streets or on the freeway with complete docility. The explosion comes when you stuff your foot down on the gas pedal, either on purpose or accidentally.

The car squirts forward like an unleashed dragster, the four exhaust pipes give a throbbing bellow, and suddenly you're way above the speed limit with an aura of cold sweat on your forehead."

Road Test concluded: "For the street drag racer, who doesn't mind sinking close to 6 grand in his toy, the 440 Six-Pack or the 426 Hemi will be very hard to beat in the Stop Light Grand Prix. . . . The Challenger is good looking, comfortable, and handles extremely well. . . . With a huge number of possible combinations, there is no reason there can't be a Challenger in your future!"

And yes, the Challenger sold well enough that it saw the light of day in 1971, though sales for the 1970 E-body Barracuda and Challenger were only 64 percent of the 200,000 per year Bert Bouwkamp had promised.

Dodge wisely made very few changes for the next year, so if you liked the '70 Challenger, the '71 was just fine. However, total Challengers built for 1971 were 27,377, or less than 36 percent of 1970's sales. "We lost money on the program and I was lucky to keep my job as director of product planning," Bouwkamp said. "It seemed like every time John Riccardo [Chrysler's President] saw an E-body he got mad at me. Instead of a promotion to VP, I got a new boss [George Butts], who was newly appointed the VP of Product Planning. In 1974 we discontinued Barracuda and Challenger." Maybe the Challenger *was* too late to the ponycar party?

At least this '71 Challenger R/T from The Brothers Collection brought loads of entertainment to the party. Option code E87 gives it the 440 six-pack delivering Hemi-like power at lower cost and less maintenance. Just 250 buyers in '71 chose this engine, 129 with four-speed, 121 with TorqueFlite. The 727 TorqueFlite three-speed makes it a joy to drive, giving up almost nothing to the four-speed stick, and the Super

Continued on page 177

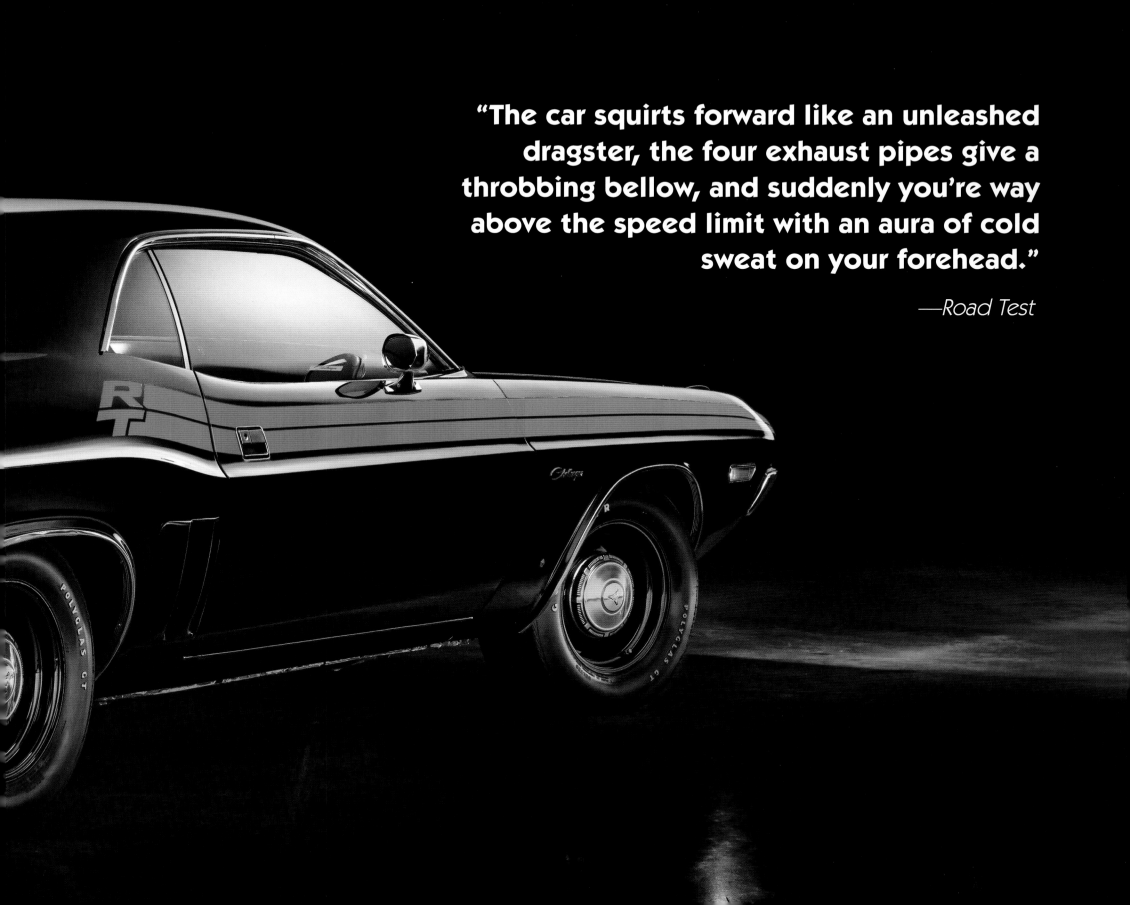

"The car squirts forward like an unleashed dragster, the four exhaust pipes give a throbbing bellow, and suddenly you're way above the speed limit with an aura of cold sweat on your forehead."

—*Road Test*

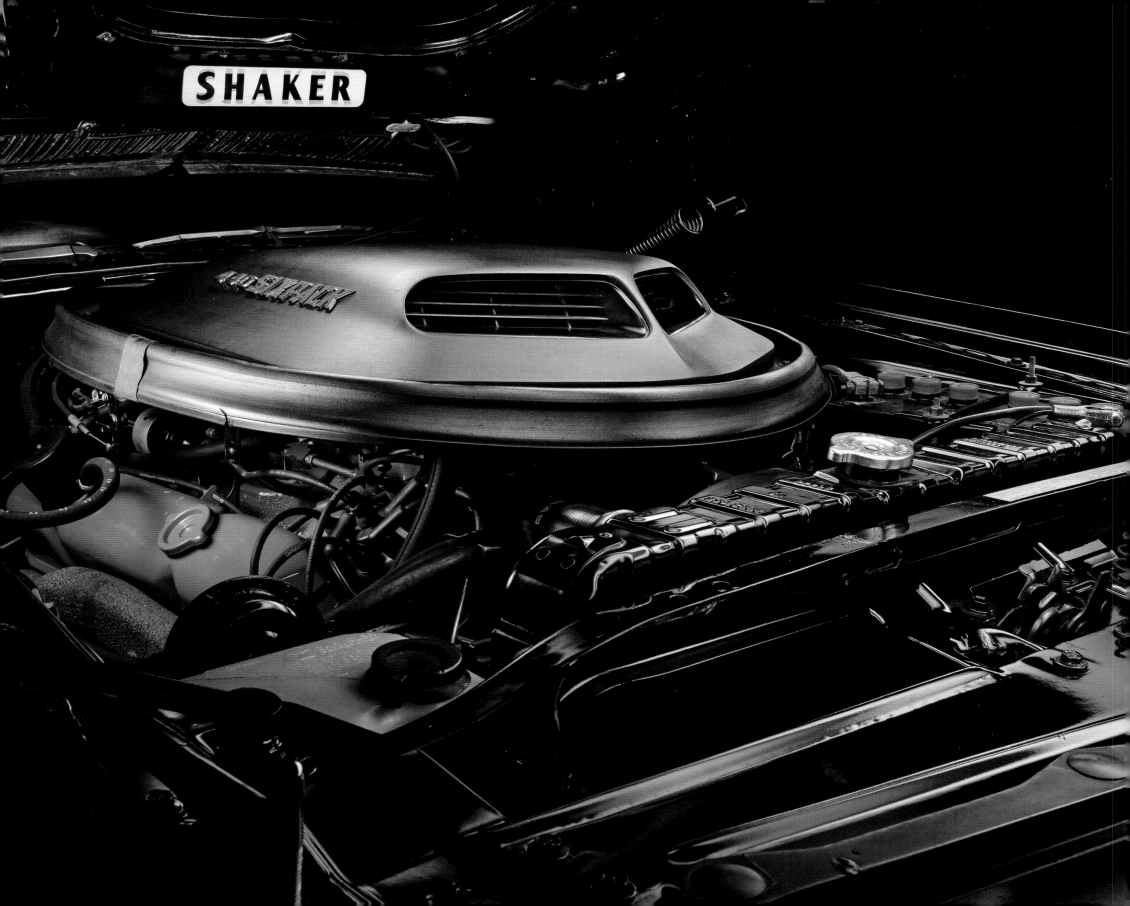

Continued from page 173

Track Pak with a bulletproof 4.10:1 Dana 60 makes it literally leap off the line. Goodyear Polyglas F60-15 tires were the biggest you could get from the factory, and the painted steel wheels with dog dish caps were the strongest, lightest available.

Power steering and brakes are a necessity with the big, heavy engine up front, and the rallye gauges keep tabs on everything. It's dressed up with TX9 Tuxedo Black paint and the very rare V6V Orange R/T stripes just to make a statement. Finally, the Challenger is topped off with the famous, functional Shaker Hood.

One option is missing: the radio. It's really not needed. Chrysler said the Shaker Hood "puts on a song and dance right before everyone's eyes." In this 440+6 Challenger R/T, that's more than enough entertainment.

CHAPTER TWENTY-ONE

PRODUCTION 58

OPTIONS

E74 426 Hemi ($789.95)

D21 Manual 4-Speed
Transmission ($198.10)

A34 Super Track Pak
($201.75)

W34 Collapsible Spare
($12.55)

TX9 Black Paint

H6X9 Black Vinyl Interior

V9W White R/T Stripes

V1X Black Vinyl Top ($82.40)

HORSEPOWER

425 at 5,000 rpm

TORQUE

490 at 4,000 rpm

1971 DODGE CHALLENGER R/T HEMI FROM MR. NORM'S

If someone wanted to buy their dream Dodge back in the muscle era, where would you go? Your local dealer? He might have a nice performance car in the showroom to draw traffic, but that might be it. And that dealer's salesmen probably knew all about Dodge's family sedans and workhorse trucks, but next to nothing about performance machines. No, for that dream car, all roads led to Chicago.

As teenagers in the forties, Norm Kraus and his brother, Len, began working at their father's gas station on the corner of Grand Avenue and Spaulding Street, making three cents per gallon pumping gas, checking fluids, and cleaning windshields.

In 1956 at age twenty-two, Norm, and Len, decided to try selling used cars on the corner of their dad's gas station and made a tidy $60 profit on the first car they flipped. Then a 1956 Chevy Bel Air convertible came into the dealer equipped with 265 V-8 and three-speed manual gearbox. They placed a classified ad in the paper and, with space at a premium, wrote "call Mr. Norm" on the ad. "The next morning I must have had 25 calls," Kraus told *Hemmings*. "By 10 a.m. I had already delivered it. By 11, my brother, who was out buying cars, called me and I said, 'Do not buy a regular car again. Buy all four-speeds.' We got an education in performance from our customers."

With their reputation well known, Dodge approached Norm and Len about opening a dealership. At first skeptical due to the huge drop in Chrysler product sales, in 1962, at age twenty-eight, Norm Kraus became the youngest Dodge dealer in America. "I think the first month we sold about thirty-five cars," he said. "From that day on, it was totally performance." The legend of Mr. Norm's Grand Spaulding Dodge was born.

By 1963 a brand new dealership building was on the corner of Grand and Spaulding. In 1964 a Clayton chassis dynamometer was installed. After seeing inconsistent performance from the factory, Norm decided, "Every high-performance customer is going to get a free dyno tune. When we sold a high-performance car, we had the car dyno'ed right in front of the customer. When completed, the dyno man would put a dyno sticker on the left rear quarter glass. The car was then taken to the prep area where everything was checked out including the installation of special-ordered performance equipment [wheels, tires, headers, hi-rise manifold, headers, gears, etc.]. When completed, a Mr. Norm's Sport Club members sticker was installed on the right rear lower glass or upon request the front lower right side glass. Finally the car was brought in front to be delivered to the customer with a key tag, T-shirt, and a license plate frame. Then the customer was showed all the equipment that was installed and how to operate the vehicle. I came out when available and personally thanked the customer and let him know the sale did not stop there and assured him we were there for any service necessary." It was that kind of special customer service that helped Mr. Norm's sell half of the performance Dodges in the United States. *Half!*

That dyno man was normally Gary Dyer, Mr. Norm's ace engine tuner and driver of the Grand Spaulding Dodge Funny Cars. In 1964, "a racer asked if he could put 'Grand Spaulding Dodge' on the side of his car in exchange for some spare parts," Norm Kraus recalled. "The next Monday we sold

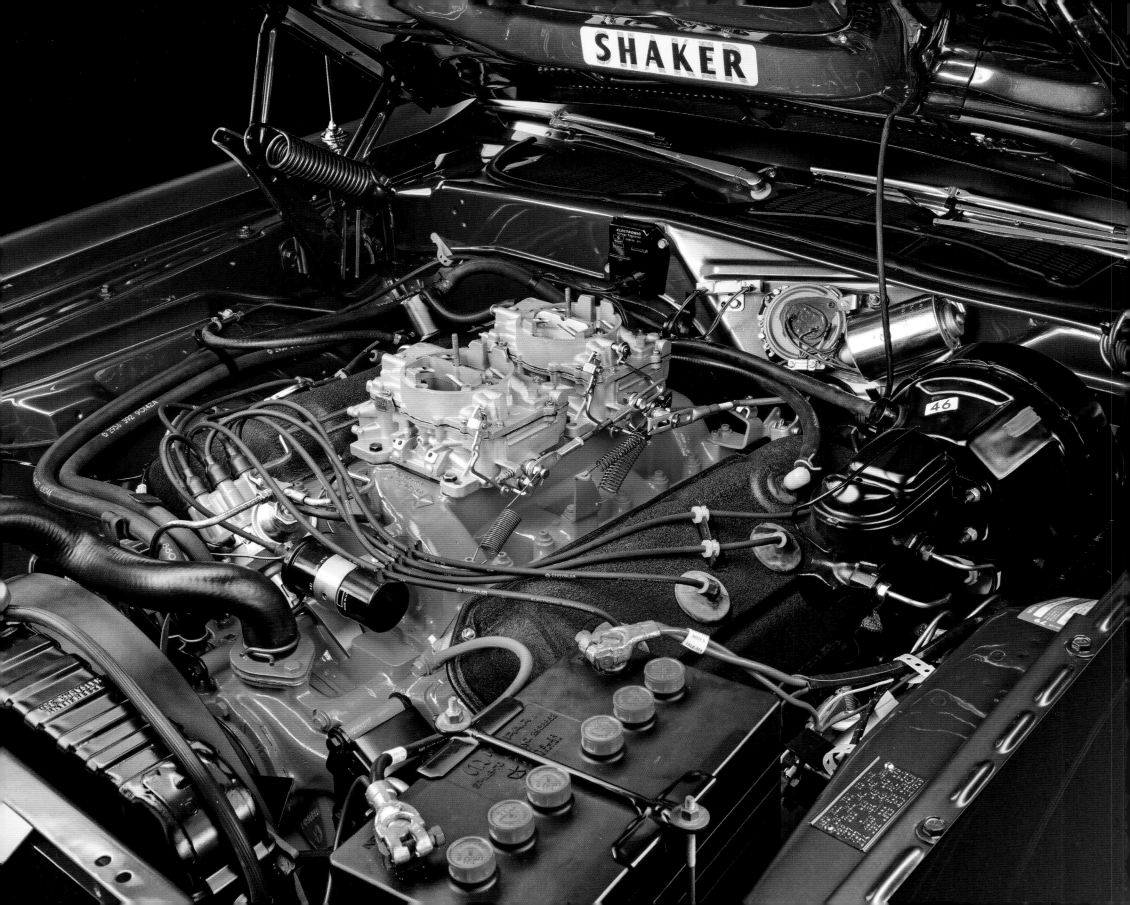

MR. NORM - THE RAM CHARGER KING - SAYS:

"WHEREVER YOU LIVE - I'LL PAY YOUR FARE FROM ANYWHERE!"

Join the GO GROUP

Mr. Norm
THE RAM CHARGER KING

With A Great New HEMI-RAM!

THE ONLY PRODUCTION CAR IN AMERICA GUARANTEED TO RUN IN THE 11's -- RIGHT OFF THE SHOWROOM FLOOR!

MEMBER NORM'S SPORT CLUB

DRIVE A "RAM" - JOIN MR. NORM'S SPORT CLUB - & ENJOY THESE IMPORTANT BENEFITS:
• DISCOUNT ON ALL PARTS
• 1,000 & 4,000 MILE TUNE-UPS (Labor Only)
• SUBSCRIPTION TO DRAG NEWS
• ATTEND GRAND-SPAULDING DODGE SOCIAL EVENTS
• ENTER MR. NORM'S SPORTS EVENTS FOR PRIZES & TROPHIES
• ATTEND MR. NORM'S SPORTS CAR CLINIC

IMMEDIATE DELIVERY

➤ HEMI-RAMS
➤ RAM CHARGERS
➤ STREET RAMS & 383's
➤ 4-SPEEDS & AUTOMATICS!
➤ ALL BODY STYLES!

$20,000 HI-PERFORMANCE PARTS IN STOCK!
PHONE & MAIL ORDERS ACCEPTED

MR. NORM'S BULLETIN BOARD
* * * * * * *
JUNE 28th
SPECIAL EVENTS FOR MR. NORM'S SPORT CLUB MEMBERS - AT OSWEGO!
CASH PRIZES & TROPHIES!

GRAND-SPAULDING DODGE
3300 W. GRAND AVE., CHICAGO Phone CA 7-3300

something like five cars." Starting the next year, the racing relationship with Kraus and Dyer lasted until 1973. By then, Grand Spaulding Dodge was the largest Dodge dealer in the world. But as a sign of the times, the dealership wasn't making their sales on performance cars any more, but on the new craze of conversion vans.

Painted Code FC7 "Plum Crazy," the triple-black 1971 Dodge Challenger R/T Hemi in The Brothers Collection was purchased new from Mr. Norm's and has all the documentation to prove it. It's equipped with the Pistol-Grip four-speed, along with the Super Track Pak with 4.10:1 gears and Dana 60 axle, so you know what it was built for. The Challenger is mostly original, but had

the Hemi short block replaced under warranty. Considering the rough life this Challenger must have had initially, the car's condition is amazing. Just fifty-eight Hemi four-speed Challengers were built in 1971.

Available from 1970 to 1971, Plum Crazy was one of the optional High Impact Paints (HIP) that were very popular at the time—so popular Dodge revived it in 2007 for today's Challengers and Chargers. It's the perfect color choice for a Hemi Challenger purchased at "The Hi-Performance Car King," Mr. Norm's Grand Spaulding Dodge. With a Challenger this awesome, who wouldn't want the whole world to see it?

"Inside the streamlined shell, it can be anything from a Casper racer. . . . With the huge number of possible combinations,

Milquetoast transportation car up to a real air-grabbing street there is no reason there can't be a Challenger in your future!"

—Road Test

CHAPTER TWENTY-TWO

1971 PLYMOUTH HEMI 'CUDA COUPE

PRODUCTION 48

OPTIONS

E74 426 Hemi Engine
($883.90)

D34 TorqueFlite 3-Speed
Automatic ($209.00)

A01 Light Package ($35.75)

A34 Super Drag Pack
($210.75)

B51 Power Brakes ($41.55)

C16 Console ($53.05)

J45 Hood Pins ($15.20)

L31 Fender-Mounted Turn
Signals ($10.70)

N96 Shaker Hood Fresh Air
Package (N/C)

N97 Noise Reduction Package
(N/C)

R11 Solid-State AM Radio
($61.10)

EV2 Tor-Red High Impact
Paint ($13.85)

H6X9 Black Vinyl Bucket Seats

HORSEPOWER

425 at 5,000 rpm

TORQUE

490 at 4,000 rpm

November 25, 1970, was the day before Thanksgiving, but for someone in Concord, California, Christmas came a month early. That's the day this Hemi 'Cuda coupe was delivered to Freeway Chrysler-Plymouth. It has all the goodies—425-horsepower Hemi, TorqueFlite automatic, 4.10:1 Dana 60 rear—but not too many other options. According to the data plate, it was even supposed to have the huge black "billboard" stripes that covered the rear quarter panels on 1971 models, which would have shouted "Hemi," yet they were never installed. Everyone could see this was one special automobile—though no one could know just how special it was going to be.

From a distance, it seemed like the 1970 'Cuda rolled into the '71 model year with few alterations. Detroit was still of the mindset of making annual styling changes. Did the beautiful '70 Barracuda really need an upgrade? Well, it got one anyway, and the single headlights that differentiated the Barracuda from the upscale Challenger were gone, with both cars having quads now. Then there was the new grille, "designed to suggest barracuda fish teeth," said Diran Yazejian, plus on the 'Cuda models the front fenders' "simulated chrome inset louvers suggested gills."

Under the hood, the same engines offered in 1970 were available in the Barracuda, starting with the thrifty

196-cubic-inch slant-six. Performance 'Cuda models started with the strong 340 and went from there. But in preparation for the upcoming unleaded fuels, all engines received lower compression ratios, and about a 5-horsepower loss. All engines except the 426 Hemi, which was untouched.

Since the first Race Hemi engines were created in 1964, all 426 Hemi engines were lovingly built at Chrysler's Marine and Industrial Engine Division facility in Marysville, Michigan, about 55 miles north of Highland Park. This plant converted Chrysler's engines into special marine applications and for industrial uses. In fact, by 1965, Chrysler had 29 percent of the US marine engine market. Low-volume but very high-quality engines were the focus of this operation—the perfect home for the legendary 426 Hemi to be built. During the Street Hemi's lifetime, the only major modification was the introduction of hydraulic valve lifters in 1970, which reduced some of the maintenance this engine required. In all, Marysville produced around 11,000 Street Hemis starting in 1966. Chrysler's mighty Trenton Engine Plant could produce that many engines in no time at all, but the 426 Hemi was no mass-produced engine. Even at an $833 option in 1971, Chrysler likely lost money on every one, yet they could justify it on the reputation this powerplant created—nothing less than the King of the Road.

But the times were rapidly changing. "Pony cars are where most performance engines find a home and these, as is becoming well known, are looked upon with considerable disfavor, in combination with their usually youthful buyers, by insurance companies," wrote *Motor Trend* in their 1971 Buyers Guide. "The all new Barracuda appeared last year just when these companies became aware they could spot (and avoid) a performance-minded client not just by the cubic inches of the car he owned, but by the specific model designations and a calculation new to

Hartford called power-to-weight ratio. A nearly deaf and blind, and, perhaps senile, octogenarian with a 500-cubic-inch 375-horsepower Cadillac Eldorado is considered a far better risk than a recent graduate who sinks his savings and most of his weekly paycheck into a 440-cubic-inch six-pack 'Cuda of about the same horsepower." Based on that magic formula, a 340 'Cuda or 383 Road Runner would be tolerated, but any engine larger than that could cost a small fortune for insurance, that is if you had a clean record. Get one or two tickets and the insurance burden could be unbearable.

Don't blame the insurance companies entirely. The onus of government emissions, safety, and fuel economy regulations dramatically changed the way Chrysler Engineering had to operate, and performance was no longer a consideration. One other factor came into play: the baby boomers were maturing, and young families needed different transportation. But the precipitous drop in sales of Plymouth's E-body cars was still a shock: from 54,800 in 1970 to 18,690 in 1971.

The last year of a Barracuda convertible would be 1971. The 440 six-barrel also got the ax. Then on June 18, 1971, a Dodge Charger left the factory with the last 426 Hemi ever built.

That Tor-Red 'Cuda in Concord, California, was just one of forty-eight Hemi automatics built that year and would be pampered its entire life. Today the 'Cuda is one of the jewels of The Brothers Collections and, except for a few filters and hoses, is exactly the way it was delivered that November day in 1970.

Special indeed!

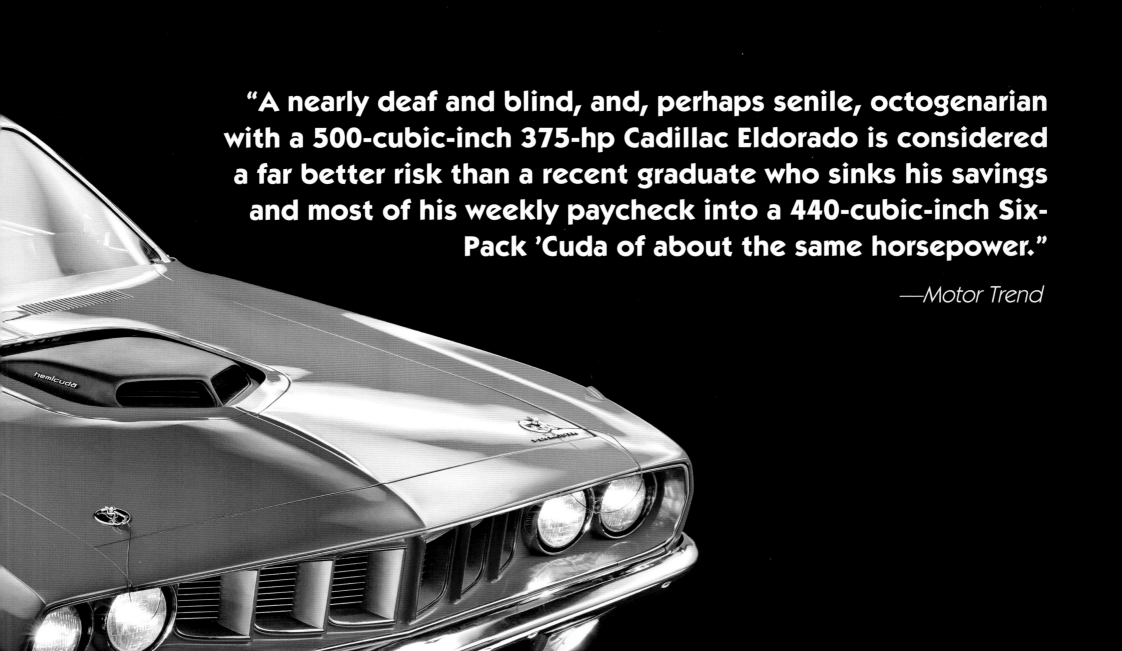

"A nearly deaf and blind, and, perhaps senile, octogenarian with a 500-cubic-inch 375-hp Cadillac Eldorado is considered a far better risk than a recent graduate who sinks his savings and most of his weekly paycheck into a 440-cubic-inch Six-Pack 'Cuda of about the same horsepower."

—*Motor Trend*

CHAPTER TWENTY-THREE

1972 PLYMOUTH ROAD RUNNER GTX 440+6

PRODUCTION

1

OPTIONS

E87 440+6 Engine
($262.15 in 1971)

D34 TorqueFlite 3-Speed
Automatic ($244.65)

H41 Strato Ventilation
($18.20)

M51 Power Sunroof ($469.65)

N96 Air Grabber Hood
($71.00)

R26 AM/FM Cassette
($225.70)

FE5 Rallye Red Paint

D6X9 Black Vinyl Bucket Seats

V1X Black Vinyl Top

HORSEPOWER

385 at 4,700 rpm (in 1971)

TORQUE

490 at 3,200 rpm (in 1971)

After the runaway success of the 1968–1970 Road Runner, creating the next generation would be a huge challenge for Plymouth. For designer John Herlitz, "That would have been about 1967, and we sold the design for the Satellite and Road Runner in late '68. Then I was promoted to studio manager in charge of the intermediate cars," he told *Collectible Automobile* magazine. Herlitz had helped design the fuselage look that all Chrysler products were embracing, and with its rounded curves and "loop" front bumper/grille, it was a radical departure, " . . . although I set up the face of the facelifted 1970 to kind of lay the tracks, lay the groundwork, for what was going to happen with the all new car for the next year," Herlitz said.

The shock was too much for some Plymouth lovers and it took a while for them to warm up to the '71 cars. But for the folks at *Hi-Performance CARS* magazine, it was love at first

sight: "While the car and its concept was immediately accepted by the supercar set, it wasn't so graciously received by our test staff—until 1971. The Road Runner became one of those cars that just never made it with us. We had felt the early models were too boxy, extremely tasteless, and sported an interior that had been rejected by the Taxi division. . . . For 1971 the Road Runner is a whole new ball game."

Hi-Performance CARS continued about the '71 Road Runner: "On the quarter the Road Runner handled quite well and performed better than we had expected. We didn't touch the plugs, distributor or even play with tire pressures. . . . The first few runs netted us with 100 mph time slips with E.T.'s averaging around 14.30 seconds. Good respectable street performance. After we had mastered the 'easy off the line' technique, we got the E.T.'s down to the 13.80's with top speed in the 102

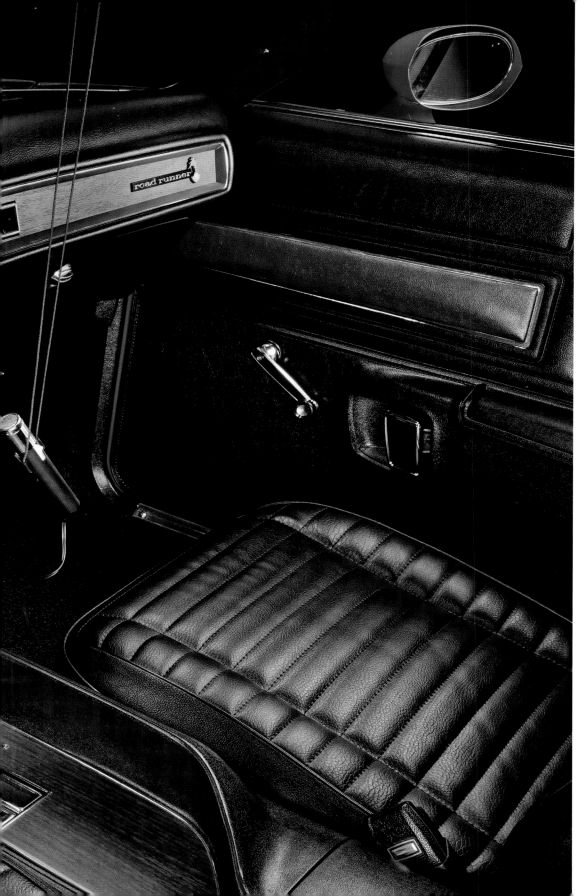

bracket." The magazine would have preferred a fixed hood scoop over the Air Grabber, though: "The only function it really serves is for goofing at a traffic light." It also thought the stripe treatment was a bit much: "It looks as though the Jolly Green Giant walked over the car and left his footprints." But those are minor points. "It took us a few years longer to fall in love with the Road Runner, but we think it was worth waiting for, *Hi-Performance CARS* added. "It's a looker, a goer, and a handler. Now if they could just bring back the $3,000 price tag." *Hi-Performance CARS* wasn't the only Road Runner fan in '71; it was also *Road Test Magazine*'s US Car of the Year.

Though the 1971 Road Runner was a great car with many improvements, sales were a paltry 13,046, and just 2,626 were of the more upscale GTX. For 1972, the Road Runner and GTX were combined. Road Runners were available with 340 and the new 400 engines, but when the power came from a 440, it was called a Road Runner GTX. The only real change externally was different taillights and rear bumper. Under the hood, all engines got reduced compression in preparation for the mandated unleaded fuels that were coming. Bumping the venerable 383 to 400 cubic inches offset some of those losses.

As a sure sign of the times, the legendary 426 Hemi was no longer offered. Give Chrysler credit: the race-bred Hemi would not tolerate a reduction in compression, and rather than castrate the "Elephant," they dropped it completely. The truth is that demand for the Hemi trailed off to just eighty-five B-body Plymouths in '71, another victim of the skyrocketing rates insurance companies were slamming Hemi cars with.

Continued on page 201

"We had felt the early models were too boxy, extremely tasteless, and sported an interior that had been rejected by the Taxi division. . . . For 1971 the Road Runner is a whole new ball game."

—Hi-Performance CARS

Continued from page 197

Another causality of 1972 was the 440 six-barrel. Well, almost. Check all the books, read all the magazines, and Chrysler did not offer the 440 six-barrel engine in 1972. But it seems as many as three 440 six-barrel cars slipped through for 1972, including one Road Runner GTX with power sunroof. This one. The transition from one model year to another wasn't always clean, especially if the changes from one year to another were minor. Leftover parts from the previous year were used up on the first few new cars, or if parts ran out, new model parts were used on the last of the previous year's vehicles. This might have been the case with the '72 six-barrel.

It's a real shame, since a '72 Road Runner GTX packing 440 six-barrel firepower would have been another masculine muscle machine, though slightly less potent than before. As it was, the '72 440+6 Road Runner GTX, now residing in The Brothers Collection, marks the swan song of Chrysler's muscle car era.

CHAPTER TWENTY-FOUR

1980 KENNY BERNSTEIN PLYMOUTH ARROW FUNNY CAR

PRODUCTION

1

OPTIONS

None

HORSEPOWER

2,500 at 8,000 rpm

TORQUE

Unknown

Most masterpieces hang on a wall. Not Kenny Bernstein's.

When Kenny Bernstein decided to go drag racing he chose the ultra-competitive Funny Car class. He did so in the absolute state-of-the-art, cost-be-damned machine you see here, the Budweiser King.

Kenny Bernstein drag raced Top Fuel cars in the Texas area in the late sixties, then left racing completely to devote all his energy to building a chain of seventeen "Chelsea Street Pub" restaurants in Texas and the Southwest. By 1978 Bernstein's business was very successful, and he was ready to go racing again—with a vengeance.

Choosing the Funny Car class meant competing in the most popular professional class at the time. Back then the nitromethane-fueled machines could hit 245 miles per hour in the quarter mile, and most events saw close to fifty

Funny Cars competing for sixteen qualifying spots. Ever the overachiever, Bernstein determined to build the best machine possible. The legendary California engine builder, Ed Pink, began with a cutting-edge chassis built by H & H Racecraft. A fiberglass Plymouth Arrow body was chosen over a wide variety of Funny Car bodies available back then since this shape seemed to have less aerodynamic drag and more downforce over the others. The Arrow was covered in Candy Apple Red by Bill Carter of Northridge, California, while Glen Weisgerber in New Jersey applied the gold leaf lettering, and Bernstein's new Kenworth tractor-trailer hauler was painted to match. Bernstein dubbed the beautiful machine the "Chelsea King" after the marque sandwich in his restaurants.

Under the "flopper" body was a 480-cubic-inch Hemi built by Ed Pink using aluminum Keith Black block and heads, with a big 8-71 blower and Enderle injectors. Running on nitromethane, the engine produced around 2,500 horsepower delivered through a Crowerglide clutch and Lenco two-speed transmission. Despite the stiff competition in Funny Car, Bernstein and the "Chelsea King" defeated future legend John Force for his first National Hot Rod Association (NHRA) victory at the 1979 Gator Nationals with a 6.45 second/233.76 mile per hour run, and was Funny Car champion in the competing International Hot Rod Association (IHRA) that same year.

When the '79 Gator Nationals in Baton Rouge, Louisiana, were postponed a week due to rain, Bernstein and his team headed for St. Louis, Missouri. Bernstein parked his gorgeous hauler and race car in front of the Anheuser-Busch headquarters, and made a pitch for Budweiser sponsorship. The 1980 season began a partnership with "The King of Beers," and the "Chelsea King" Arrow was now the "Budweiser King." Again, Bernstein chose the best to update his racer—famed drag racing artist Kenny Youngblood created the car's striking graphics. Thus began Bernstein's thirty-year association with Budweiser, which ultimately exceeded Richard Petty's twenty-eight years with STP, and John Force's twenty-nine years with Castrol.

In 1981 it was time to replace the original "Budweiser King" with a newer "King," again adorned with a similar paint scheme. By 1985 Bernstein would be NHRA Funny Car champion, which he would earn three more times. Then in 1990 Bernstein switched to the Top Fuel class, where he captured two more championships for Budweiser, and became the first driver to exceed 300 miles per hour in the quarter mile. Along the way he also established a NASCAR team, which earned three Winston Cup victories from 1988 to 1995. A CART open wheel team was also formed, and Roberto Guerrero sat on the pole of the 1992 Indianapolis 500 in Bernstein's ride.

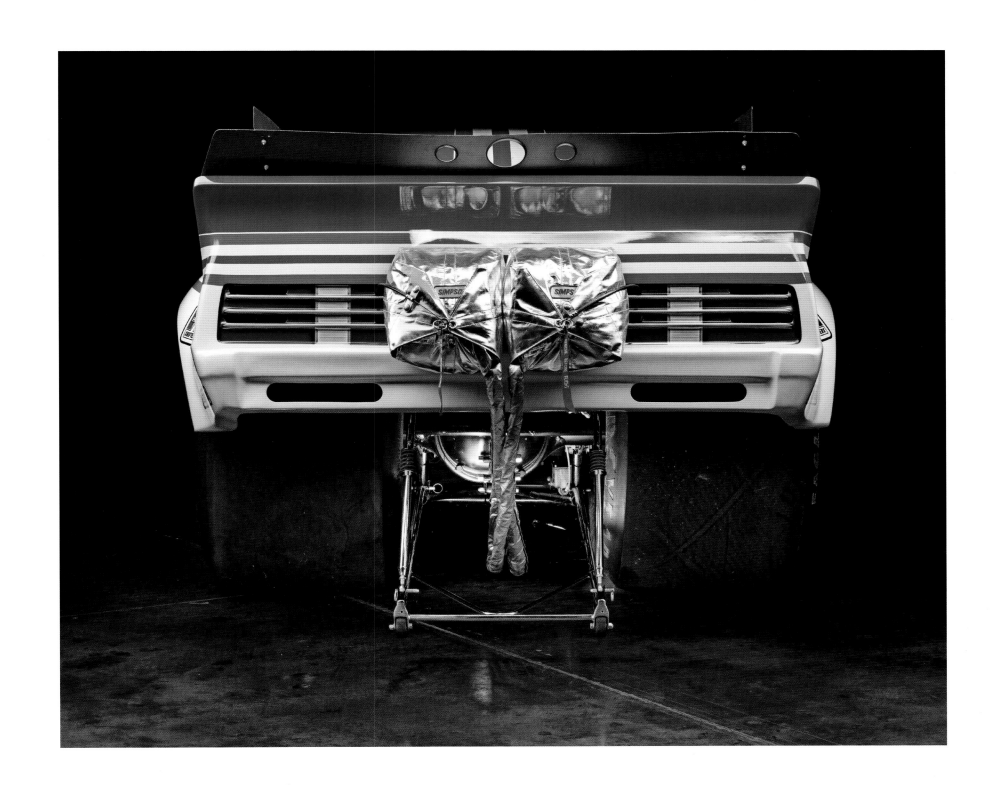

Kenny Bernstein finally retired as a driver in 2002, and as a team owner in 2011, the only owner to record victories in NHRA, NASCAR, and Indy Cars. The original "Budweiser King" was sold in 1983 to a racer in Montana who drag raced it locally. It was sold again in 2004 to someone who recognized the historical significance of this Funny Car, and restored it to its original equipment and condition.

The sport of drag racing has changed much since Kenny Bernstein built this Funny Car in 1978. Today, the strip is one thousand feet, and Funny Cars travel it in less that 3.9 seconds, topping out at over 330 miles per hour. But the heart of just about every Funny Car and Top Fuel dragster since the mid-seventies has been the 426 Hemi. Today these 500-cubic-inch engines generate 11,000 horsepower, with 90 percent nitromethane forced into the engine at 110 gallons per minute. It's estimated it takes 950 horsepower just to turn the supercharger at full throttle, and the twin sparkplugs throw a spark equivalent to an arc welder to ignite the dense explosive fuel mixture. Still, open up one of these $150,000 engines, and the block and cylinder head design is clearly based on the legendary 426 Hemi—huge valves, twin rocker shafts, and hemispherical combustion chambers. True, these powerplants are bigger, stronger, and purpose-built for the fastest racers on the planet, but rest assured they are still a Hemi at heart, even if the valve covers say Chevrolet, Ford, or Toyota.

As the "Father of the Hemi," Tom Hoover, told this author in 1994: "When you watch a Top Fueler run 300-plus miles per hour today, what more can I say. That says it all!"

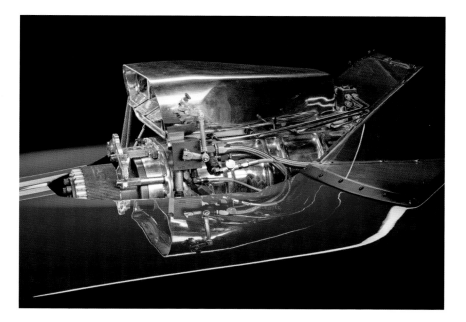

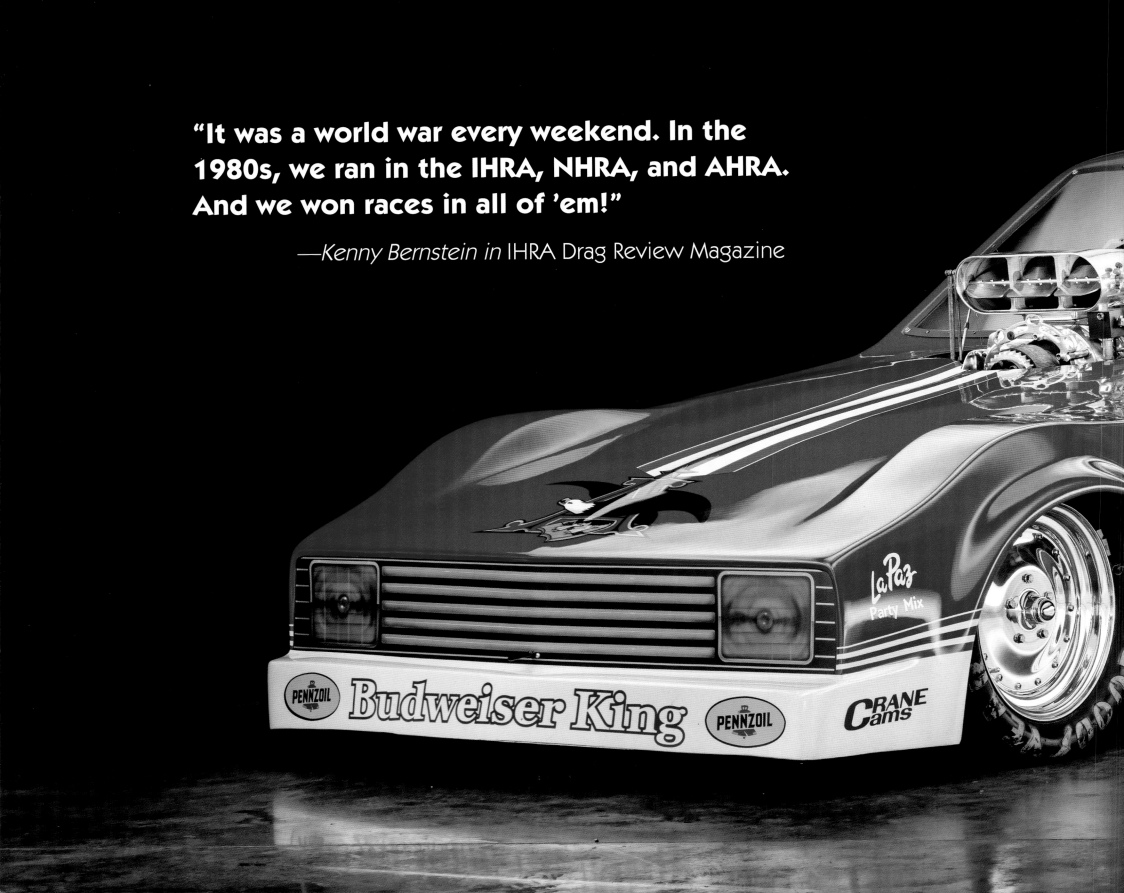

"It was a world war every weekend. In the 1980s, we ran in the IHRA, NHRA, and AHRA. And we won races in all of 'em!"

—Kenny Bernstein in IHRA Drag Review Magazine

CHAPTER TWENTY-FIVE

2016 DODGE CHALLENGER SRT HELLCAT

PRODUCTION

11,995

OPTIONS

TorqueFlite 8-Speed Automatic
HP90 Transmission

HORSEPOWER

707 at 6,000 rpm

TORQUE

650 at 4,000 rpm

Never is a long time, but by the mid-seventies, it seemed like the epic muscle era would never return. Even America's sports car, the Corvette, had just 165 horsepower under the hood in 1975, and when a gallon of regular gas crossed the $1 mark around 1978, that sealed the deal.

There were glimmers of hope with every new Mustang, Camaro, or Firebird released, but not much there for Mopar fans. Then in 2002, Daimler Chrysler released the third-generation Hemi engine in trucks, and the Chrysler 300 and Dodge Magnum and Charger came a few years later. But would there ever be a King of the Hill, like the legendary 426 Hemi?

First, the 2008 Dodge Challenger was released. Designer Michael Castiglone of Chrysler's Pacifica Advanced Design Studio in California incorporated many design clues from the 1970 Challenger into his concept. Like the E-body cars

that were derived from the B-bodies, Chrysler Engineering shortened the Charger's LX platform by 4 inches and made other changes to create the LC body uniquely for the Challenger. "During the development of the concept car, we brought an actual 1970 Challenger into the studio," Castiglone said. "For me, that car symbolizes the most passionate era of automotive design."

Inside, another young designer from the Pacifica Studio, Allen Barrington, sought clues from the original Challenger. "It's just an extreme, emotional car, so we tried to just capture that, but in a new way," he said. "Like on the interior, the Pistol Grip shifter, things that people remember about those cars that were very unique, especially to the Mopars, that I just wanted to capture in a new way using new materials and more geometric shapes and forms."

Hot Rod magazine dove into the third-generation Hemi engine: "The massive power potential is inherent in the Hemi's opposed-valve design, allowing space for large, free-breathing ports with a direct shot into the cylinder. The production iron 426 Hemi heads were cavernous and delivered approximately 300 cfm of intake airflow—a stout number for that era. The latest third-generation Hemi heads easily eclipse the stock 426 Hemi's airflow. On top of the airflow, these modern heads come stock with fast-burning twin-plug chambers, a shallower valve angle for greatly reduced combustion chamber volume, and twin active quench pads adjacent to the valves. The engineers did their homework here, taking the two-valve Hemi layout to what may be its optimal form." Chrysler even brought in retired 426 Hemi engineer Tom Hoover to consult on the design.

The new Challenger was a really fine performance machine, with excellent handling characteristics to go with the third-gen Hemi power, but the full potential was not reached until . . .

"The new Challenger SRT Hellcat captured the title the 'FASTEST MUSCLE CAR EVER' with a National Hot Rod Association–certified quarter-mile elapsed time of 11.2 seconds at 125 miles per hour (mph) with stock Pirelli P275/40ZR20 P Zero tires. With drag radials, the run dropped to just 10.8 seconds at 126 mph." That news bombshell on July 11, 2014, made it official: The new King had just been crowned!

Pulling a reliable 707 horses out of the new Hemi was more than just a basic hot rod operation. SRT Powertrain Director Chris Cowland explained, "The increased peak cylinder pressure of the Hemi Hellcat required that pistons, conrods, and crankshaft were all upgraded. The pistons are forged high-strength alloy, and the piston pins use diamond-like carbon coating. Ninety-one percent of the content is new." And on top of that engine was an intercooled supercharger displacing 2,300cc and flowing 30,000 liters of air per minute—

enough to suck the air from a 10x13-foot room in sixty seconds, Dodge engineers said. Remember, this is 707 *net* horsepower. By comparison, using the SAE Gross horsepower ratings of the sixties, this would be closer to 1,000 horsepower!

Aerodynamics are critical on a projectile capable of 199 miles per hour right off the showroom floor. "In the case of the 2015 Challenger SRT Hellcat, many hours were spent in the wind tunnel to make sure each platform remained stable at terminal velocity," wrote Steve Magnante in Dodge's *Redline* blog. "Chin and trunk spoilers were fine-tuned, under-car belly pans massaged and fascias reconfigured to slip through the air stream without excess drag or lift. But what about the hood? The aero team came up with a novel design incorporating a group of precisely positioned openings. The trio of openings are there to cool the engine bay and enhance aerodynamics."

Along with the rarest, most desirable automobiles from the muscle era in The Brothers Collection, their 2016 Dodge Challenger SRT Hellcat fits right in: B5 Blue paint, 707 horses, 8-Speed Automatic, 199 miles per hour, eleven-second quarters. Extreme. Emotional. No question, the new King of the Hill belongs with these legends.

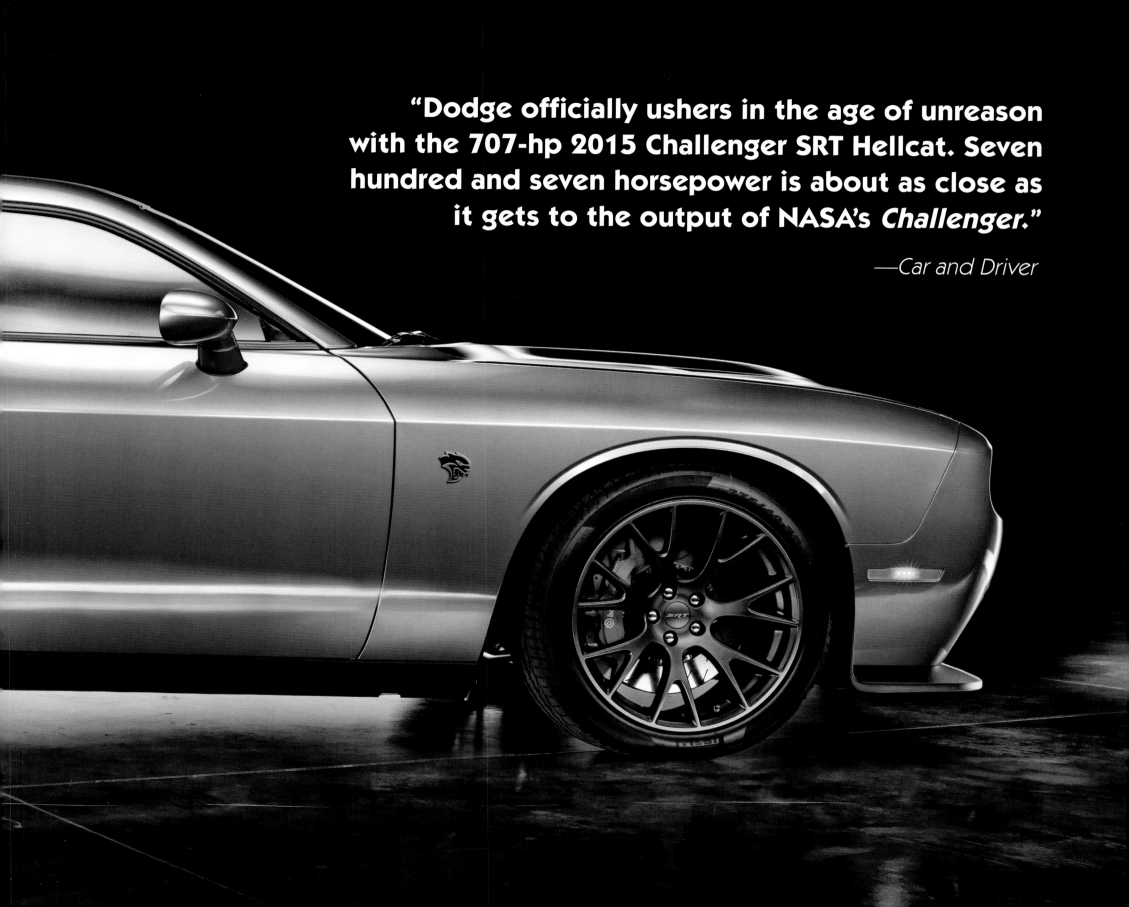

"Dodge officially ushers in the age of unreason with the 707-hp 2015 Challenger SRT Hellcat. Seven hundred and seven horsepower is about as close as it gets to the output of NASA's *Challenger*."

—*Car and Driver*

PHOTOGRAPHER'S NOTES

Car photographers have several techniques we can use to "light" the car. I probably am best known as a "light-painting" shooter. Light-painting vehicles is very different from lighting them in a studio with a massive overhead soft box and reflectors. As light-painting maestro Dave Wendt describes it, the process is more organic. I'd add "spontaneous" as well. When I first started this lighting style, I used a small soft box or even a hardware store work light with an incandescent bulb in it. The lights gave me the control I needed to shine the light on the car to create the image I envisioned. But incandescent bulbs are hot and hard to work with and the bulbs constantly burn out. Throughout

the shoot, if electric power surged or dropped, I had color-shift problems. I tried to use LEDs but they gave me an uneven look with streaks of light in the reflections. I tried other types of lighting to improve the process. I wanted to be cordless, flexible, have even light over the vehicle, and find a lightweight setup that would be easy to handle.

After years of testing light sources I finally found the perfect light system. Cineo Lighting, located in Half Moon Bay, California, manufactures small, easy-to-work-with battery-powered lamps with correct and constant light temperature. Their lamps use remote phosphor technology, not LEDs. Cineo

has—for me—the perfect-sized light units to make the perfect image. I shot this entire book using Cineo Lighting gear. You can learn more about them at their website (www.cineolighting.com). For me, they are a dream come true: portable, cordless, color-correct, lightweight, with a comfortable operating temperature. Cineo Lights made these shoots easier, faster, and safer. They gave me incredible consistency unlike anything I've used before and offer much more light than even a 200-watt incandescent bulb in a soft box.

The technique is deceptively straightforward. First, of course, you need a spectacular car in front you in a room or outside location with no extraneous light. As for shooting, lock the camera in place on a tripod, focus it, and set the exposure (depending on the length of the vehicle) for somewhere between 8 and 15 seconds. Typically I use an aperture between f/11 and f/16—I adjust these exposures as I see the results. I turn on the light in my hand, turn out the room lights, open the camera shutter, and walk past the car at a steady speed with the light at a constant distance from the vehicle. The shutter closes. I do it again, back and forth across the vehicle, twenty or thirty times (more about this later).

Whatever I do, I do *not* touch the camera during any of this activity—pixel-to-pixel registration is essential for image assembly.

Every time I see the image in my monitor, I'm amazed. Light streaks appear along the most beautiful character lines of the vehicle—its rooflines and rocker panels, its fenders and even engines. Why twenty or thirty passes? Make a pass with the light at ankle height, knee height, waist height, chest height, head height, and even overhead. Try letting the light rise and fall with the fender or roof contours. Then change from one Cineo Light—the Match Stix—to the Match Box. Then do it all over again.

With my previous lighting (soft boxes with incandescent light bulbs) I was constantly tripping over extension cords and stumbling into the cars or walls or other obstacles. The manageable Cineo lights allow me to easily and safely maneuver around, along, and over the car I'm shooting. The only thing I need to do is place a piece of tape over the power-on light; this prevents unwanted streaks of light from appearing in my image. Cineo Lighting offers soft boxes for some of their lights as well as barn doors for their Match Stix. These lights offer just about the right amount of illumination and freedom needed to make this process work. Over time, I can imagine how the car will look after each pass.

A friend introduced me to the CamRanger. This electronic device lets a photographer operate his modern-day auto-everything camera equipment by remote control. My friend fired his camera using his iPad mounted on a tripod, but he had to walk to see the image after each light pass. I prefer to use my iPhone because it saves time. I can modify aperture, shutter time, and even wirelessly adjust focus on autofocus lenses. The benefit of this is I can light-paint without an assistant to "push the button." With my iPhone, I saw nearly instantly whether I'd succeeded or failed. I shoot RAW but the CamRanger

works quickly with small jpegs so I reset my Nikon D810 to take both.

A friend likened his early experiences lightpainting to learning to play three-dimensional chess wearing a blindfold. He could think about what he was doing but had no idea what it looked like, even when he could see his most recent exposure on the CamRanger screen. His advice was, "Shoot and keep shooting. Be sure you have enough passes." I'll add: when you believe you are done, start all over again and shoot more. This is not an obsessive-compulsive speaking but a recommendation borne from experience from one who did not follow important advice early and often.

I established a production goal of shooting two or three cars in each ten- or eleven-hour day, five days a week. This meant a side profile view, a ¾ front, a ¾ rear, an engine view or two, and details. This proved ambitious, and I built up hundreds of files that were waiting for me to edit when I got home.

But did those exposures—or the dozen or more that I made—give me what I needed to define, describe, or sculpt vehicle in question? When I got to the computer and began stitching the views together was the moment of truth.

I've used Adobe Photoshop for years and made primary adjustments in color balance, contrast, shadow, and highlight preservation. As a light-painter, this was only the beginning. At this point in the process, it was all about the choices I made and those I was facing. Each light pass gave me a different feel or look. Remember, each pass is a different layer in Photoshop. Hopefully the end result—the book you are now holding—proves I made the right choices.

INDEX